LANDSCAPING

TIME LIFE BOOKS

This volume is part of a series offering home owners detailed instructions on repairs, construction and improvements which they can undertake themselves.

HOME REPAIR
AND IMPROVEMENT

LANDSCAPING

BY THE EDITORS OF
TIME-LIFE BOOKS

TIME-LIFE BOOKS
AMSTERDAM

TIME-LIFE BOOKS

EUROPEAN EDITOR: Kit van Tulleken
Assistant European Editor: Gillian Moore
Design Director: Ed Skyner
Photography Director: Pamela Marke
Chief of Research: Vanessa Kramer
Chief Sub-Editor: Ilse Gray

HOME REPAIR AND IMPROVEMENT

EDITORIAL STAFF FOR LANDSCAPING
Editor: John Paul Porter
Deputy Editor: William Frankel
Designer: Edward Frank
Associate Editors: Mark M. Steele, Brooke C. Stoddard
Text Editors: Lynn R. Addison, William Worsley
Staff Writers: Kevin D. Armstrong, Patricia C. Bangs,
Deborah Berger-Turnbull, Carol Jane Corner, Rachel
Cox, Leon Greene, Kathleen M. Kiely, Victoria W.
Monks, Kirk Y. Saunders
Copy Co-ordinators: Stephen G. Hyslop, Diane Ullius
Art Assistants: George Bell, Fred Holz, Lorraine D.
Rivard, Peter C. Simmons
Editorial Assistant: Myrna E. Traylor
Picture Co-ordinator: Renée DeSandies
Special Contributors: William Doyle, Lydia Preston,
David Thiemann

EUROPEAN EDITION
Series Director: Jackie Matthews
Editor: Lynn Earnshaw
Designer: Paul Reeves
Sub-Editors: Frances Dixon, Jane Hawker, Hilary
Hockman
Special Contributor: Liz Hodgson

EDITORIAL PRODUCTION
Production Assistants: Nikki Allen, Maureen Kelly
Editorial Department: Theresa John, Debra Lelliott

ISBN 7054 0800 0

TIME-LIFE is a trademark of Time Incorporated U.S.A.

THE CONSULTANTS: Robert Holden is an associate of a London firm of
landscape architects and chairman of the South-East Chapter of the
Landscape Institute. Formerly a lecturer at Thames Polytechnic School
of Architecture and Landscape, he also has landscaping experience in
Europe and the Middle East.

John Bungey, a member of the Australian Institute of Horticulture Inc.
and of the Royal Australian Institute of Parks and Recreation, has
received numerous awards for his garden designs and landscape projects.

Contents

1 Organizing the Outdoors

Analysing the earth. In a soil test, a sample of garden earth in the bottom of a syringe is exposed to a chemical that will help disclose its composition. Each such chemical (available in test kits at garden centres) changes colour when it mixes with the soil. Colour charts that come with the kits are matched with the coloured chemicals in order to determine the soil's concentrations of such nutrient elements as nitrogen, potassium (indicated in the form of potash, a potassium compound) and phosphorus.

There was a time when the word "landscaping" evoked images of immaculate lawns and elegant gardens, designed by landscape architects and meticulously maintained by platoons of gardeners and nurserymen. But times have changed. Today, many of the landscaping principles and techniques that have been used for centuries to beautify parks and estates are converting suburban plots and tiny town house gardens into pleasant, functional environments—without professional help and often at surprisingly low cost.

Landscaping is simply the organization of outdoor space to provide much the same sort of amenities—privacy, comfort, beauty and ease of maintenance—that are built into the interior of a home. Just as the inside of a house can be modified by basic woodworking, plumbing and wiring skills, so the land around it can be reshaped by the techniques demonstrated in this volume: clearing and levelling earth; planting and nurturing lawns, shrubs, trees, climbing plants and flowers; and assembling or building such structures as garden pools, rock gardens and trellises or pergolas. It is possible, in fact, to plan a garden as a kind of oversized family room, with walls of hedges and fences; ceilings of sky, shade trees and pergolas; and floors of grasses and ground covers. A comprehensive landscaping plan includes all of these elements, along with such decorative additions as flower beds and man-made ornaments, from a modest fountain to a terraced swimming pool.

A good plan *(pages 16–21)* not only meets individual tastes and requirements, but takes the uniqueness of the land itself into consideration. No two pieces of land are exactly the same, even when their dimensions and the houses built upon them are identical. A garden may be overgrown or barren, level or uneven, sunlit or shaded, moist or dry. The site may originally have been an ancient swamp, forest or farmland, with soil enriched by natural or chemical fertilizers—or it may be a rocky outcrop filled with rubble, in which only the hardiest plants will grow. It is as important to know the limitations of your land as it is to know its potential. Simple tests *(pages 32–33)* tell whether the soil is sandy, clayey or loamy, and kits like the one shown on the opposite page reveal the chemistry of the soil—the presence of basic nutrients, and the degree of acidity or alkalinity.

Fortunately, most deficiencies are correctable. Armed with the right tools *(pages 8–11)*, even a novice can remove rocks and stumps, level ridges and hollows, grade slopes, dig drainage ditches, erect retaining walls, and enrich the soil or alter its chemistry to encourage plant growth. With these preparations completed, a landscaping plan can be made a reality, transforming your speck of the earth's surface into an enclosure of singular beauty and utility.

A Landscaper's Tool Kit

Like every other craft, landscaping calls for specialized tools. Some, such as those shown here, are in frequent use; others, such as those shown on pages 10–11, are needed less often. An amateur landscaper should consider buying all or most of the tools in this first group (they are listed below according to function).

HAND GARDENING. A trowel, hand fork and weeding fork are used for individual plants and flower beds.

PRUNING AND TRIMMING. A pair of secateurs can sever branches up to 10 mm thick; lopping shears can slice branches up to 25 mm thick; still larger limbs are trimmed with a curved, coarse-toothed pruning saw. High branches can be cut with tree pruners, which have a pulley-operated cutter and a removable saw blade. Ragged shrubs should be trimmed with scissor-like hedge clippers.

DIGGING. A spade with a sharp blade is ideal for many landscaping tasks, such as digging and turning soil, and cutting through turf and roots. A shovel is used for mixing and moving earth and other loose materials, such as bark chippings. A fork turns compost and moist soil, both of which stick to spades.

TILLING. The most common tool for cultivating the soil is a Dutch hoe; a bow hoe or cultivator, useful for working in confined spaces, will break up the soil further. A longspan rake levels and smooths the earth in preparation for planting.

WEEDING. A push-pull weeder will remove weeds from between plants without disturbing them. Large-scale weed clearing requires a weed trimmer, a petrol or electric-powered machine with a whipping nylon line that mows weed or grass tufts. A springtine lawn rake sweeps up light debris, such as dead weeds or grass trimmings, while an edging knife's straight blade cuts through turf round pathways and flower beds.

SPRAYING. A garden-hose sprayer dilutes a concentrated solution as it squirts out of a nozzle. Caution: keep separate, labelled sprayers for fertilizer and for insecticide or herbicide.

TREE PRUNERS

WEEDING FORK

FORK

TROWEL

HAND FORK

HEDGE CLIPPERS

SHOVEL

SPADE

WEED TRIMMER

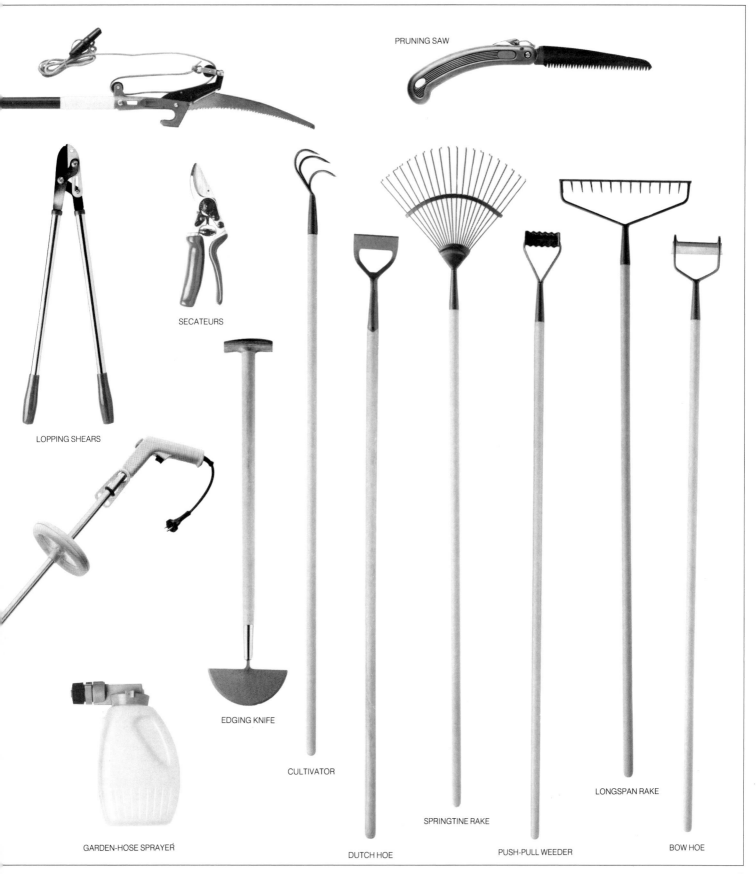

PRUNING SAW

SECATEURS

LOPPING SHEARS

EDGING KNIFE

CULTIVATOR

GARDEN-HOSE SPRAYER

DUTCH HOE

SPRINGTINE RAKE

PUSH-PULL WEEDER

LONGSPAN RAKE

BOW HOE

9

Special Tools for Rare Jobs

Landscaping tasks that come up infrequently sometimes call for tools designed expressly for the job. Such single-purpose tools need not form part of your basic tool kit. Hand tools can be purchased co-operatively by several gardeners in a neighbourhood; large tools and petrol-driven machines are available for hire from tool rental shops.

BOW SAW. This single-handed saw is used for cutting limbs from small trees and making felling cuts in tree-trunks.

BULB PLANTER. Simply a cylindrical trowel, this tool extracts a core of soil, leaving a hole for bulbs or small plants.

PRESSURIZED KNAPSACK SPRAYER. Powered by a hand pump that compresses air over a liquid, this pressurized sprayer provides pinpoint application for small amounts of solution.

SCARIFIER. Suitable for small lawns, this barb-tined rake has blunt teeth that comb out the build-up of dead grass that can otherwise choke a lawn.

HOLLOW TINE AERATOR. Operated by pushing the tines into the ground with a foot on the crosspiece, the hollow tine aerator removes plugs of earth from compacted soil and lawns.

HEDGE TRIMMER. Electric-powered saw blades speed up large hedge trimming and other cutting tasks.

LAWN ROLLER. Filled with water or sand, the hollow drum compacts soil and levels lawns.

TROUGH SPREADER. The trough can contain grass seed or powdered fertilizer, which is dropped evenly as the spreader moves across the ground.

POWER AERATOR. Tines on a rolling drum slash holes in earth or turf from a lawn, allowing air and nutrients to penetrate hard-packed soil.

POWER CULTIVATOR. Rotating blades break up packed soil or mix compost and conditioners into the soil. The machine illustrated is the same one as the aerator, with the tines replaced by blades.

SCARIFIER

HOLLOW TINE AERATOR

BOW SAW

BULB PLANTER

PRESSURIZED
KNAPSACK SPRAYER

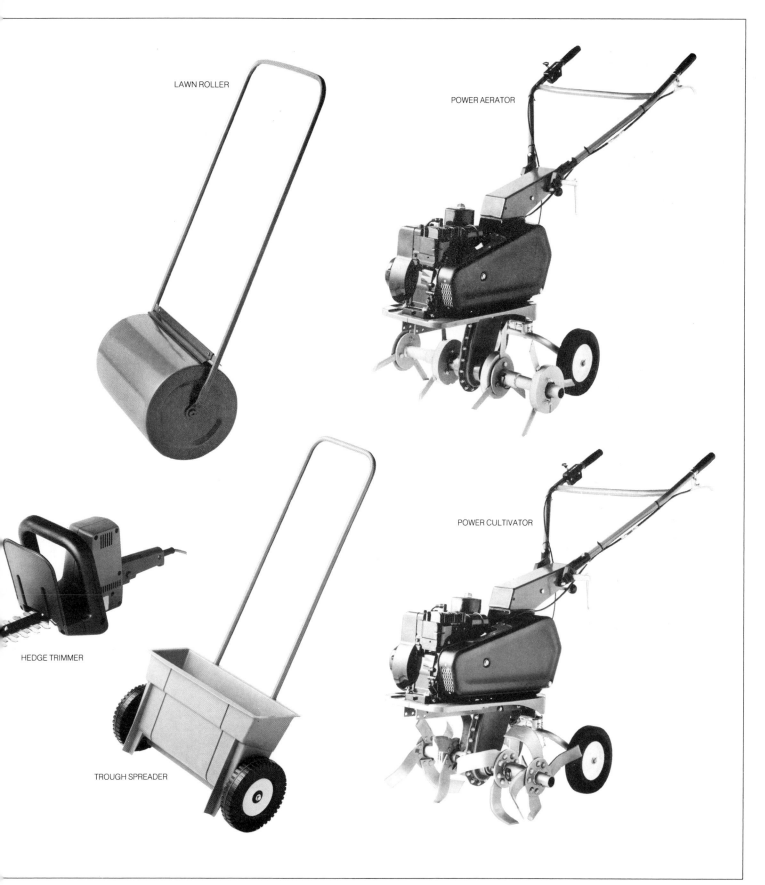

LAWN ROLLER

POWER AERATOR

HEDGE TRIMMER

TROUGH SPREADER

POWER CULTIVATOR

The Care and Repair of Landscaping Tools

A collection of gardening equipment represents a substantial investment, which needs and deserves protection. Common-sense maintenance begins with periodic inspections to catch minor scratches and loose joints before they grow into major problems. At times, repairs are in order when handles break or hoses split; except for such inexpensive tools as trowels and bamboo lawn rakes, a repair almost always costs less than a replacement.

How you store your tools in the shed, garage or basement is an important part of their maintenance. Keep all your tools under cover, and relatively free of dust and rust-producing moisture. A wall covering of pegboard fitted with hooks to hold tools by their handles is an ideal arrangement; it keeps sharp blades away from hard, damp floors and secures them within easy sight and reach. Roll garden hoses carefully and hang them on brackets. Label fertilizers, insecticides and herbicides and store them out of the reach of children. Rinse and dry a sprayer after each use to prevent contamination and corrosion.

Cleanliness is as important as order in the maintenance and storage of tools. Use a coarse brush and running water to get rid of mud; use steel-wool pads to remove rust from tools that were neglected during the winter months. After cleaning dirt from a cutting tool, always wipe the blade or blades thoroughly with a soft, disposable cloth which has been dampened with a few drops of light household oil. Lubricate shears and secateurs with a drop of oil on hinges and a few more on springs, then work the oil in by opening and closing the blades several times.

Sharpening the cutting edges of tools is a major part of routine tool care. Even a spade is inefficient if it is blunt, making a back-breaking chore of chopping tough roots. Fortunately, tools such as shears, spades, hoes and axes do not require professional sharpening; you can give them a good cutting edge at home with a flat file, a whetstone or—for long, curved blades—a rounded scythe stone.

Garden hoses spring leaks even when used with care. Avoid the temptation to wrap insulating tape round a punctured section; the makeshift patch will hold temporarily, but water pressure will eventually stretch the tape and the hose will begin to leak again. Bicycle-tyre repair kits are sometimes effective for mending a rubber hose, but they contain a solvent that can actually dissolve a vinyl hose. The best solution in this case is to slice out the leaking section, and then splice the hose with a mending kit *(opposite page)* available from hardware shops and garden centres. Make clean cuts with a sharp knife, then soak both of the cut ends in hot water for a few minutes; the heat will soften the vinyl, which makes it much easier to fit the hose end over the connector that comes with the mending kit.

For a loose or corroded hose-end fitting, use a replacement coupling. Installing the new coupling is simple if you have the right size and model. Hoses are sized by inside diameters; measure after cutting away the old coupling. Remember that a female coupling is connected to the water source, a male one to a nozzle or sprayer.

Sharpening Spades and Secateurs

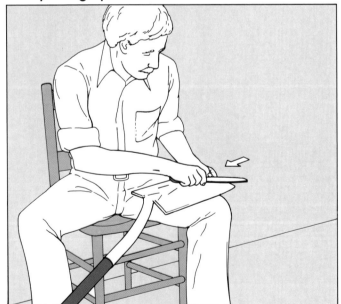

Putting a keen edge on a spade. Steady the spade on your knee, back side up, and stroke the edge of the spade with a flat file. Pull the file in long, steady strokes directed towards the centre of the blade and following the angle of the bevel. If the inside edge of the blade is also bevelled, turn the spade over and sharpen that edge.

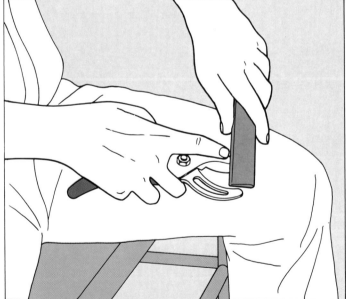

Honing a pair of secateurs. Open the secateurs and sharpen the bevelled edge of the blade with the edge of an oilstone, using a gentle circular motion. Follow the angle of the bevel carefully to avoid damaging the cutting edge of the blade.

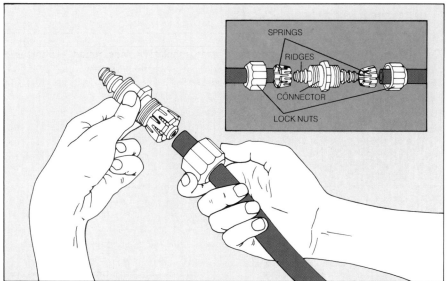

Mending a Leaky Hose

1 **Making the connection.** After cutting away the damaged section of the hose, slip one of the lock nuts from the mending kit *(inset)* over a cut end of the hose, unthreaded end first. Following manufacturer's instructions, push one end of an expanding spring over the three ridges at one end of the connector; then, for a hose with a 13 mm inside diameter, insert the first ridge of the connector into the hose *(left)*. For hoses more than 13 mm in diameter, the connector must be pushed deeper into the hose; consult the manufacturer's instructions for more exact directions.

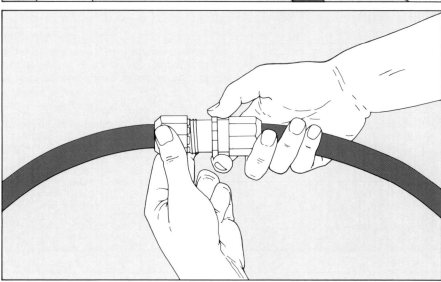

2 **Assembling the parts.** Slide the lock nut over the spring, and tighten the nut securely by hand (metal tools can damage the plastic connector). Finally, fasten the other end of the connector to the hose and tighten it.

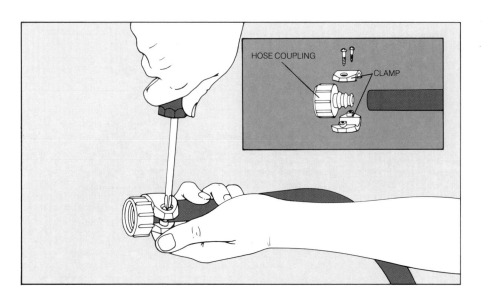

Replacing a Hose Coupling

Clamping a coupling in place. After cutting off the defective coupling, push the new coupling as far into the cut end of the hose as it will go. Then assemble the halves of the clamp round the hose and the base of the coupling *(inset)*. Match the holes in one half of the clamp with the screw receptacles in the other, then screw the halves together to tighten the clamp round the hose *(left)*.

Keeping a
Sprayer Nozzle Clean

1 Clearing the outlet holes. Wearing rubber gloves to prevent contact with any chemical residue, unscrew the spray tube and nozzle from the pistol grip *(inset)*. Clear blockages and debris from the outlet holes at the end of the spray tube with a stiff wire, then wrap the wire in paper and dispose of it immediately to make certain that it will not be used again.

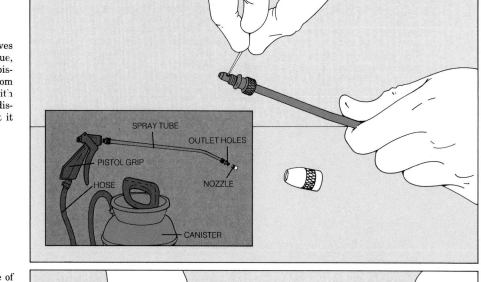

2 Cleaning the nozzle and tube. Wipe the inside of the nozzle and the threads of the spray tube with moistened cotton wool buds until the cotton comes away clean, then lubricate the inside of the nozzle and the ends of the tube with a bud dipped in light household oil. Finally, lubricate the plastic O-rings at the ends of the tube to keep them from sticking and to prolong their sealing power.

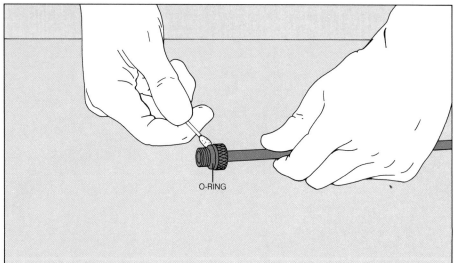

Cleaning a Garden-Hose
Sprayer

Back-flushing the sprayer head. Wearing rubber gloves, rinse the reservoir of the sprayer with clear water, and connect the sprayer head to a garden hose. Turn the control valve of the head to ON, cover the outlet hole with a finger and run water through the hose; the clean water will flush back through and out of the suction tube, washing away chemical residues. Remove your finger from the outlet hole and run water through the sprayer in the normal direction; if the hole is clogged, clear it with stiff wire.

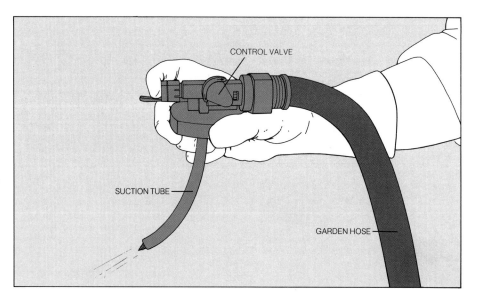

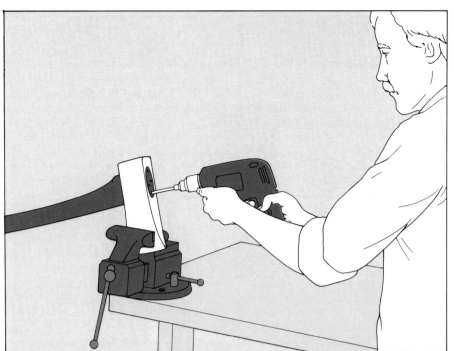

A New Handle for a Large Tool

1 **Removing a damaged handle.** Secure the head of a large tool, such as the axe shown here, in a metalworker's vice. Drill four deep holes into the wood at the top of the handle, using an electric drill with a 6 mm bit; locate the holes as close as possible to the edges of the wood. Remove the tool from the vice, and tap the head with a small sledge hammer, driving it down towards the narrow part of the handle. If the head remains stuck, drill additional holes and tap more vigorously.

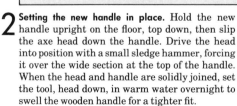

2 **Setting the new handle in place.** Hold the new handle upright on the floor, top down, then slip the axe head down the handle. Drive the head into position with a small sledge hammer, forcing it over the wide section at the top of the handle. When the head and handle are solidly joined, set the tool, head down, in warm water overnight to swell the wooden handle for a tighter fit.

3 **Making a tight fit.** Let the wood dry, then drive a 12 mm metal wedge, available at hardware shops, into the top of the handle. If the head of the tool is even slightly loose on the handle, drive additional wedges—perpendicular to the first—until the head is absolutely secure.

How to Be Your Own Landscape Architect

Like any other home improvement, landscaping calls for advance planning. Even a small garden is amazingly flexible, and the design imposed upon it is dictated largely by personal tastes and individual needs. Be prepared, then, to experiment on paper, weighing alternative solutions to your problems and sketching numerous possible designs. A thorough job in the planning stage not only assures you of a garden in which you can take pride and pleasure, but also saves the time and money it takes to compensate for hastily made decisions.

Begin by assessing the existing garden. A plan showing the size and shape of the property, such as the example shown on the opposite page, above, is all but indispensable at this stage.

Leasehold properties will usually have a surveyor's plan which can be used as a base for your plan. Freeholders in urban areas will often be able to consult official large-scale maps which show details of individual properties. Failing this, measure out the dimensions of the plot yourself, and transfer them to a scale plan as shown on the opposite page.

On your plan, include all the elements suggested in the example. Local water, gas and electricity boards will indicate the position of underground pipelines and cables that might interfere with your construction projects. If you are not sure of the direction of prevailing summer and winter winds, contact either the national or regional Meteorological Office.

With a clear picture of the garden, you can determine the changes or additions that must be made to meet your needs. Draw up a list of these needs, based upon the activities you are planning for your garden. Most outdoor areas are used for a variety of purposes—work, play, relaxation—and the best gardens have distinct areas for activities that might conflict. The plan on the opposite page, below, shows outlines for several use areas, located according to a universally accepted rule of residential landscape design—the most logical spot for an outdoor use area is next to the part of the house from which the area will be entered.

To some extent, the orientation of a house on its plot of land defines these areas. Traditionally, the house divides the plot into an approach area in the front; a private living area at the back; and an out-of-the-way service area, perhaps at the side of the house, for such storage facilities as a tool shed or a set of dustbins. A logical place for decoration would be the approach area at the front door, where passers-by and arriving guests can appreciate it. A storage area would be situated near a garage; a patio or terrace for outdoor relaxation might be located directly outside French windows or patio doors leading from the living room to the back garden. An area for games, on the other hand, should obviously be situated as far as possible from any windows or greenhouses.

Once you have chosen and outlined use areas on your plan, experiment with preliminary designs for each one. Keep your ideas fairly general at this stage; for example, if you decide to plant shrubs or a hedge in or around an area, think of them simply as tall or short, and as green or colourful, rather than stopping to choose a particular variety. Selecting the specific plants is the last step in the design process, and this step is best undertaken with the aid of the charts on pages 53, 59, 63, 82–83, 94–95 and 115, at a point when you know exactly what sort of effect you want to achieve with your new plantings.

As you consider these preliminary plans, look for strategic positioning of plants and construction projects that might solve specific problems. If, for example, like most people, you value privacy in your garden, hedges, trees or fences can be used as screens against the street and neighbouring houses. Consider physical comfort in planning every area: the afternoon sun, for example, may make a patio too bright and hot to sit on for part of the day, but a strategically placed tree will filter the sunlight and lower the temperature beneath its branches. A high hedge or a row of evergreen trees will shelter a footpath from winter winds.

Think about convenience and safety. A frequently travelled path should be at least 1.5 metres wide, to accommodate two people walking along side by side. Set shrubs slightly back from the edges of paths so that they will not snag clothing or shower passers-by with dew. Paths should be well lit for safety, and paving should be as level as possible.

Consider maintenance, too. Hedges on both sides of a path may hinder snow removal in the winter; shrubs that grow too tall or too fast may need heavy and frequent pruning to prevent them from blocking a view you want to preserve.

Finally, consider the garden from an aesthetic point of view. To decide which views to enhance and which to block, tour the house interior, looking through every window, and check the views from a variety of vantage points in the garden itself. Then experiment with several arrangements of plants and constructions, using sketches like the one at the top of page 18. Your own taste, of course, is the best guide to follow, but you should be aware of certain principles of design that professional landscape architects usually follow (pages 18–21). Used separately and in combination, in traditional or unconventional styles, these design concepts will help you create a garden that is not only comfortable and functional, but also attractive.

Planning the Design

1 **Surveying the site.** On a sheet of graph paper, using a 2 cm square to represent 1 square metre, draw a plan of the plot and ground floor of the house and any other existing structures. In the example on the right, double lines represent walls, single vertical or horizontal lines represent windows, and single, angled lines represent doors.

In surveying the area outside the house, mark rainwater pipe locations; avoid positioning flower beds or paths at these points. Indicate good and bad views as seen from the windows and from several places in the garden; among these views, include the positions of neighbours' gardens and houses. Draw in existing trees, shrubs, flower beds and underground services; note such characteristics of the terrain as steep banks, level areas and spots with good drainage. Finally, indicate the position of the sun in the morning, at midday and in the late afternoon, and the direction of prevailing summer and winter winds.

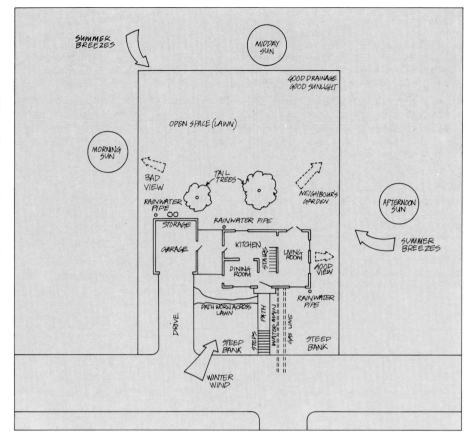

2 **Outlining use areas.** On tracing paper taped over the basic plan, outline use areas for the major sections of the garden. (For simplicity in the example on the right, only the lettering on the tracing paper is shown; in reality, the lettering on the plan would be visible through the overlay.) In the plan shown here, space accessible from both the living room and the kitchen becomes an outdoor living and dining area. The expanse of lawn behind the garage is set aside as a play area; games equipment can be stored in the garage. A back corner of the plot with good drainage and sunlight is reserved for a vegetable garden, with storage space for garden tools in an adjacent utility area. Dustbins are hidden from view behind the garage, where they are within easy reach of the kitchen door.

Smaller areas at the front of the house are also given uses, as shown in the final plan at the top of page 18. The portion of the lawn bordered by the street and the drive becomes the main approach area, and the steep bank that leads to the street is devoted to decorative plantings to block the view of the street from the living room and dining room windows.

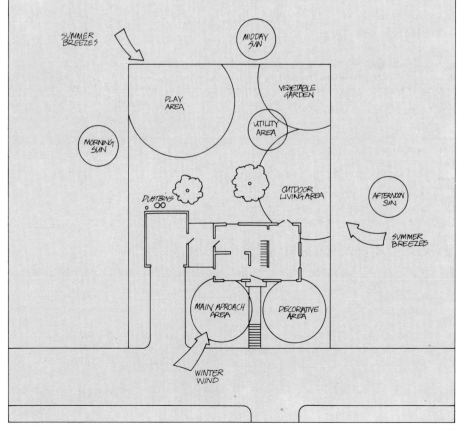

3 **Experimenting with designs.** Tape a fresh sheet of tracing paper over your plan, and experiment with designs for each of the use areas. In the example shown here, the outdoor living and dining area becomes a paved patio; new shade trees and a high hedge on the rim of the patio block the afternoon sun and the view of the neighbour's garden. The play area is left open, except for a border hedge between the garden and another undesirable view. The vegetable garden in the rear corner of the plot is bordered by fences and a flower bed; a tool shed and a row of shrubs separate the garden from the patio.

New, more efficient traffic patterns are established by a path of stepping stones between the front of the house and the dustbins, and by a paved area leading from the end of the path to the patio. In the front garden, a paved footpath runs from the drive to the front door, replacing the old path worn across the grass and the path between the door and the street. Decorative, permanent ground cover replaces hard-to-mow grass on the steep bank facing the street; the trees that block the view of the street from the house help to beautify the new approach.

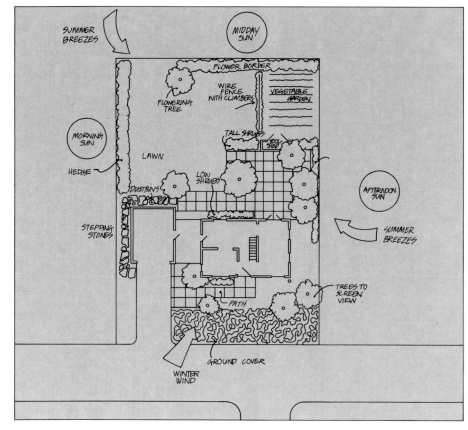

Principles of Landscape Design

Unity and balance. To meet one basic design objective, related elements in a garden are arranged to create a unified picture, in which the viewer's eye travels easily over all the vegetation. In such a design *(right, above)*, no single element stops the eye; instead, colours, textures and shapes are co-ordinated to blend and contrast as part of a larger picture, and the ensemble has a continuous, graceful silhouette.

The best way to assess the balance of a landscape is to picture it as a framed view divided vertically in half. A well-balanced design attracts your eye equally to each half; neither side overpowers the other. The halves of a symmetrically balanced design *(right, centre)* are almost mirror images; in an asymmetrical view *(right, below)*, the halves are different, but the sizes and shapes of the elements in each half are enough alike to draw the eye equally to both sides.

Focal point and proportion. Within a landscape design, a single element called the focal point may be used to attract the eye; no view should have more than one focal point. In a design for a front garden *(below)*, the front door of the house is commonly used as a focal point, and is traditionally framed by arrangements of ornamental trees, shrubs or flowers positioned so that they draw the eye towards the point of interest.

The term "proportion" refers to the relationships between the sizes of the plants and buildings in a landscape design. No set rule controls these sizes, but a height-to-width ratio of 5 to 3 between neighbouring elements is generally considered pleasing to the eye. Thus, in the example at the bottom, the tree is in proportion with the house to its left, but is too tall for the single-storeyed house on the right.

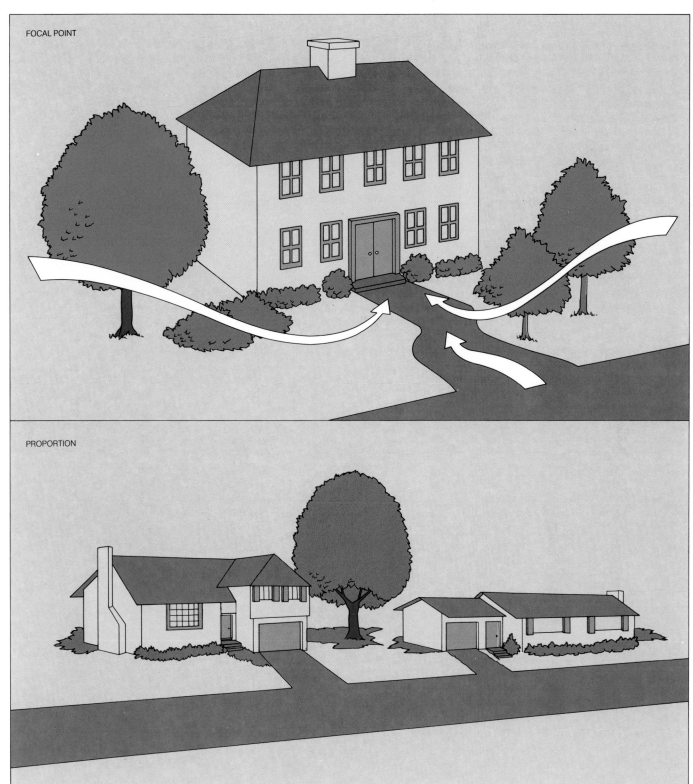

FOCAL POINT

PROPORTION

Rhythm and appeal. The repeated use of similar patterns or shapes creates a visual rhythm in a landscape design; the repetition stimulates a sense of movement by drawing the eye from one point or area to the next. In the example on the right, the openness and clarity of rectangular paving blocks and planting beds create a simple, easily grasped rhythm.

The term "appeal" refers to the element of surprise in a design and to devices that entice the viewer to explore a landscape. The example at the bottom of the page contains two such strategies. When viewed from the garden, the hidden corner of the house stimulates a viewer's curiosity about that area; when viewed from the house, the fence partially covered by ivy hides a surprise—a small stone terrace and a fountain.

RHYTHM

APPEAL

Designing with geometrical shapes. Plants and paving arranged in common, recognizable shapes give a landscape order and predictability—two features that are pleasing to the eye. Rectangles and squares *(below, top)* reflect and extend the architectural lines of a house. Circles and curves *(below, centre)* add a different kind of interest to a pattern by counterbalancing and contrasting the straight lines of the house. Triangles draw the eye to a focal point—in the example at the bottom of the page, to the expanse of lawn in the middle of the garden.

RECTANGLES AND SQUARES

CIRCLES AND CURVES

TRIANGLES

Moving Earth to Reshape the Lie of the Land

The irregular rise and fall of a naturally sloping terrain is attractive—from a distance. Except for the most rustic setting, however, uneven hollows and ridges are generally undesirable in a garden. They hinder drainage, so that lawn and garden care becomes a frustrating chore rather than a pleasant pastime; moreover, bumps and slopes make unsuitable foundations for patios or play areas. Reshaping uneven land is often an essential preliminary to a landscaping or construction project.

Shown on the following pages are techniques that transform a broken, uninviting plot into a nearly level space suitable for lawns, shrubs and trees. First, sharp inclines are levelled or terraced to prevent plants at the base of a slope from being drowned by the runoff after heavy rain. Then the newly levelled areas must be gently graded. Water will pool on perfectly level land, drowning fragile plants and flowers and making garden work impractical for several days after a downpour.

For most sites, the gentlest slope that will provide adequate drainage is 20 mm of rise for every 1.25 metres of horizontal run. If different parts of your plot slope in different directions, wait for a steady, heavy rain and observe the natural drainage patterns for an hour or so. After the weather clears, use the string-and-grid method *(pages 24–25)* to establish the right slope for each part of the plot.

Although some earth-moving jobs are extensive enough to warrant hiring an excavating company, a surprising amount of earth can be moved in short sessions of digging and hauling. If you do choose to undertake an excavating project, you will need a pair of sturdy shoes with heavy, treaded soles to ensure a good foothold and to pad the soles of your feet against the top of a spade blade. You will also need a sharp spade for skimming turf *(page 24)* and dig-ging the soil, and a heavy metal rake with a flat top for removing stones and smoothing the earth. Several stakes, a ball of string and a spirit level or line level are necessary to set the slope of your plot and mark any slope changes.

To economize effort, work when the soil is slightly moist. Wet soil is very much heavier—and therefore more difficult to move—than barely moist soil, while dry soil can be rock-hard and unyielding, even to the sharpened blade of a steel tool. A project that requires you to move only a small amount of earth from one part of the garden to another will simplify and ease the grading job; for example, you might prefer to rough-grade a slope and prevent erosion by digging a few trenches for French drains *(page 26)*, rather than undertake the large-scale and laborious job of building a retaining wall *(pages 28–31)*.

To avoid a strained back—the most common injury in this type of work—use your arms and legs as well as your back to lift a spade *(opposite)*. Use a wheelbarrow or other lifting aid whenever practical to transfer earth from one spot to another or to lift heavy loads.

If a job seems more than you can handle yourself, do as much as you can in advance to lighten the workload and reduce the cost of the hired excavators. Put up fences round areas you do not want disturbed; inexpensive wire netting, which comes in large rolls and can be easily erected, is a good choice. Keep all heavy equipment out of existing or potential garden beds; the weight of the excavating machinery can compact the soil to a depth of over a metre; this will render it impervious to water and useless for planting. When fencing in trees, include enough ground to protect their root systems. Finally, keep children and pets out of the way of the excavators, and make sure that your garden and driveway are cleared of any obstacles that block access to the work area.

Regardless of who does the actual digging, it is your responsibility to locate any electricity or telephone cables, or gas, water or drainpipes beneath your land. If necessary, request local public utilities to advise you before the earthmovers arrive.

To balance out cuts and fills, quantity surveyors make a survey of differences in elevation and soil volume, and then professional excavators systematically bring cavities up to the level of the slope with earth taken from ridges and hillocks. Few of the domestic digging projects that you can tackle yourself are extensive enough to warrant the expense of such a survey, but you may discover half way through the work that you have too much or too little soil and must pay someone to take soil away or deliver more.

If professional excavators are reshaping your garden, agree upon the disposal of excess soil before digging begins. Some contractors take it as part of their job to remove the excess, while others tack on an additional fee; moreover, you may want to keep any extra soil for use elsewhere.

If you need to purchase earth to finish a slope, be sure to gauge your order according to your needs. A cubic metre of soil will cover 40 square metres of ground to a depth of 25 mm. Buy topsoil—a mix of earth and fertilizers from which stones, wood chips and weeds have been removed—rather than fill, which often contains rocks and lumps of rock-riddled clay. Turfs need a minimum of 100 mm of topsoil to grow properly. Newly-sown seeds will need about 150 mm, and ground covers and shrubs about 400 mm. Ask a local nursery for sources of good quality soil in your area; topsoil of poor quality may be contaminated by invisible weed seeds, disease germs and fungus spores.

The Right Way to Wield a Spade

A four-stage action. Standing upright, set your foot on top of the blade of the spade *(first picture)* and force the blade deep into the earth. Step back, put your hands in the positions shown in the second picture and, bending from the waist, force the top of the handle down, using the tool as a lever to dislodge the soil. Flex your knees and slide your lower hand down the handle for better leverage; then, using your arms, back and legs together, lift and pitch the soil *(third and fourth pictures)*. To save strength, work slowly and try to avoid overloading the spade.

Managing Heavy Loads with Minimal Strain

A two-handed lift. Holding your torso straight, squat as close as possible to the load to be lifted *(far left)*. Holding the load close to your body, stand up slowly *(centre)*; in this stage of the lift, keep your pelvis tucked forwards and use your legs—not your back—for lifting force. To lessen strain on your back, continue to hold the load close to your waist *(right)*, and move your entire body, not just your torso, when you turn.

A one-handed lift. Stand behind and to one side of the load. Bending your knees slightly and keeping your back straight, lean forward from the waist to reach the load *(far left)*. Using your legs for lifting power and keeping your shoulders level, raise your body upright to lift the load; when carrying the load, extend your free arm for balance *(right)*.

Clearing logs from a site. To move a long, evenly cylindrical log, push it on to and across three or four rollers made of wood or iron pipe. Tie a rope round the forward end of the log and pull it slowly over the rollers; as each roller comes free at the back of the log, move it to the front.

Moving rocks and stumps. Using a sturdy, rigid rod, lever large stones, stumps or other unwieldy weights on to a sheet of heavy canvas or hessian. Grasp the cloth firmly at both corners of one end and drag the object from the site.

Levelling and Grading a Plot of Land

1 **Removing turf from the surface.** Hold a sharp spade almost parallel to the ground and work it in short, jabbing strokes to separate the turf from the underlying soil. After clearing away all the turf, use the spade to scrape the soil off to a depth of 25 mm to remove roots that might later send up new, unwanted shoots.

2 **Levelling ridges and hollows.** After clearing away the turf, transfer the soil from obvious high spots in the plot to low spots. After you drop each load, use the end of the blade to break the soil into chunks 25 mm wide or less.

3 **Setting a slope with stakes and strings.** Drive stakes at the four corners of the plot; the stakes at the lowest points (generally furthest from the house) should be tall enough to set their tops roughly level with those at the highest points. Tie a string to one of the higher stakes and stretch it along the side of the plot to a lower stake. As a helper checks the string with a spirit level or a line level, raise or lower the string as necessary to level it. Mark the lower stake at the level of the string, then move the string down this stake to set the desired slope *(page 22)* and tie it to the stake at this position.

Repeat the procedure on the other side of the plot, then complete the boundary by tying levelled strings between the stakes at the top and the bottom of the plot.

4 **Laying out a grid.** Drive stakes at 2 metre intervals just outside the strings marking the boundaries of the plot, then make a grid over the area by tying a string between opposite pairs of stakes at the level of the boundary strings. Make sure the strings are taut; if necessary, smooth the soil beneath them so that the strings clear the soil.

5 **Grading the surface.** Working in one 2 metre square at a time, use a heavy rake to break up the soil to the consistency of coarse sand and spread it parallel to the plane of the string grid. Finally, smooth the plot with the flat top side of the rake; remove the stakes and strings.

Correcting Faulty Drainage with Underground Pipes

To professional landscapers, "drainage" has two meanings: the seepage of water into the soil and the flow of water away from a particular stretch of land. Soil that is too porous does not hold water long enough for plants to absorb it; soil that is too dense keeps water on the surface, depriving plant roots of the periodic soaking they require. Water that flows rapidly over the surface of a steep slope erodes the soil, exposing plant roots on the face of the slope and drowning or washing away plants at the foot of the slope. Water that lingers below the surface creates waterlogged ground, with soggy, hard-to-work soil in which plants cannot thrive.

To gauge porosity, dig a hole 600 mm deep and fill it with water. If the water disappears in 24 hours or less, the soil is too porous: if any water is still visible after 48 hours, the soil is too dense. Both are solved in the same way—by double digging and adding organic matter such as manure, compost or leaf mould, or an inorganic substance such as gypsum *(pages 32–35)*.

Water flow down a steep slope can be controlled by grading the surface *(pages 28–31)*, but reshaping a slope is often impractical for large areas, and destructive where valued plants are thriving. An alter-native is to install French drains—shallow trenches filled with gravel or shingle—at the top and bottom of the slope to channel water away to a nearby stream or ditch, or the soakaway described below.

More serious drainage problems demand a more drastic solution. In areas with heavy clay or damp, peaty soils, or in hollows with no other outlet, an underground piped drainage system is the most effective way of removing excess water.

Piped drains are laid in trenches—the pattern you use will depend on the shape of your plot. The herringbone pattern shown here with branching side drains and one main drain leading at a constant incline (not less than 1 in 200, but more often 1 in 100) into a soakaway, will be suitable for most gardens. Main drains should have a diameter of 100 mm, side drains about 75 mm. The depth and spacing of the trenches will vary according to the porosity of the soil *(below)*.

Pipes must be permeable to collect water from the surrounding soil. Perforated plastic pipes are the cheapest and simplest to install—they need only be cut to length and fitted together with branch fittings. Clay or concrete pipes are laid in short sections with small gaps between to allow water to enter the drain. They are more difficult to lay and keep free of silt and debris.

The major consideration is the position of the outlet. In the absence of a nearby ditch or stream, a soakaway should be built at the lowest point in the garden, as far away from the house as possible. Garden drainage should never be combined with domestic water or sewage systems—in a storm the results could be disastrous.

For most gardens, a simple, solid soakaway—a pit filled with rubble and gravel—is usually enough to allow excess rainfall to percolate slowly into the subsoil. A soakaway should always be dug above the local water table—the level at which the ground is permanently saturated. To ascertain this level, dig a test hole about 2 metres deep in the autumn, when the ground is wet but not frozen. If water flows into the hole, you have reached the water table. Do not dig a pit deeper than 2 metres without seeking professional advice.

The dimensions of a soakaway depend on size of area, local rainfall and soil conditions. If the subsoil is impervious, the pit should be deep enough to reach more porous soil below. Generally, a pit 1 metre or more deep with a surface area of 1 square metre is adequate.

A Herringbone Pattern of Drains and Ditches

Anatomy of a drainage system. A system of perforated plastic pipes is laid in a herringbone pattern in a badly drained garden. The pipes will channel water away from the soil to a solid soakaway placed at the lowest point in the garden.

The pipes are set in V-shaped trenches at a depth of 600 to 750 mm for clay soil, 750 to 900 mm for loam and 900 to 1000 mm for sandy soil. The side drains, spaced at 3 to 6 metre intervals in clay, 6 to 10 metres in loam and 15 to 18 metres in sand, are joined to the main drain at an angle of 45 degrees using branch fittings.

The main drain leads into the soakaway through a section of impermeable pipe. The soakaway is covered by a layer of upturned turfs or glass fibre matting to prevent soil washing in and causing blockages, and this is concealed by a layer of topsoil and grass. The depth of the soakaway varies according to local conditions, but the bottom of the main drain should always be at least 1 metre above the bottom of the soakaway at its entrance.

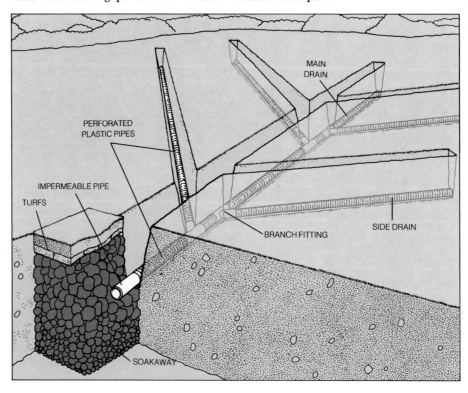

MAIN DRAIN

PERFORATED PLASTIC PIPES

IMPERMEABLE PIPE

TURFS

BRANCH FITTING

SIDE DRAIN

SOAKAWAY

Piped Drains
for Maximum Efficiency

1 Planning the layout. Starting with the main drain, mark the position of the trenches with garden twine and pegs. The main trench should be about 300 mm wide, and the side trenches about 150 mm wide; the side trenches should meet the main trench at an angle of 45 degrees.

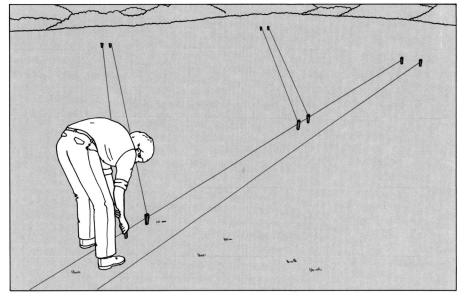

2 Digging the trenches. Carefully remove the turfs from between the marks, placing them at the side of the trench in the same order in which you have removed them. Dig trenches with sloping sides to the required depth, keeping the topsoil and subsoil separate on pieces of tarpaulin while you work. Use a spirit level to check that the slope of the trenches is constant along the whole system *(inset)*. Spread a 50 mm layer of sand and gravel in the trench as a base for the pipes.

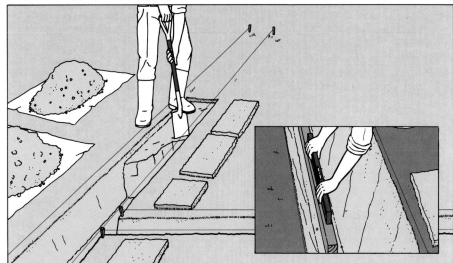

3 Laying the pipes. Starting at the lowest point, position the pipes in the centre of the trenches, bedding each one into the gravel, and attaching the side drains to the main drain with branch sleeve fittings. Use a spirit level to check the slope of each pipe as it is laid. Cover the pipes with more sand and gravel, then a layer of upturned turfs or glass fibre matting *(inset)*. Replace about half of the subsoil plus about 100 mm of topsoil and then the original turfs; tamp them down firmly.

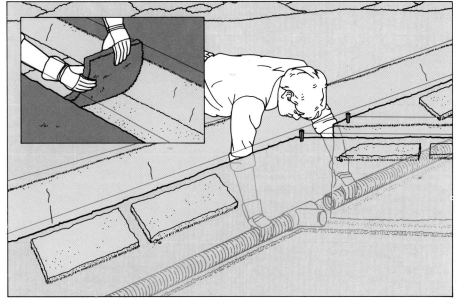

Barriers of Brick or Stone to Hold Back the Earth

Retaining walls of brick or stone have long been used by farmers to transform steep, useless hillsides into terraces of workable cropland. Nowadays, they are also valued by home owners as an element in landscape planning, lending charm to a garden and at the same time increasing the amount of useful land.

The retaining walls shown here are sturdy yet easy to build using simple masonry techniques. Like all walls they require a solid foundation, built on firm ground. In addition, their structure must be strong enough to resist the pressure of the soil behind. This pressure can be increased many times as water percolates into the soil after a fall of rain, so the structure of the wall must include holes to allow water to escape as quickly as possible.

The design shown on the following pages should not be used for walls more than 1 metre in height; to build anything higher than this requires both building regulations approval and the services of a structural engineer. On a steep slope you can build a number of low retaining walls to create a series of terraces.

Choose building materials which blend in with their surroundings—rough-hewn stone, brick or concrete blocks veneered with brick or stone. Brick walls, the easiest to build, should be at least two bricks (225 mm) thick, to support the load behind. Use exterior facing bricks made from good quality high-baked clay; for the wall shown here, you will need about 60 bricks per square metre of wall. If you are going to use hollow concrete blocks, you will need to add steel reinforcing rods to provide adequate support.

Rough-hewn stone, mortared in irregular courses and infilled with rubble and rock fragments, gives a less formal wall than block or brick. The wall is strengthened with large "tie stones" that span the thickness of the wall and bond the structure together. For extra stability, "batter" the wall—incline the sides inwards at a slope of 75 mm for every metre of height (page 31, Step 1). Use a strong mortar for a stone wall—1 part Portland cement to 3 of sand and a quarter of hydrated lime.

To anchor a retaining wall correctly, you must dig a trench deep enough to bury both the footing and at least the first two rows of bricks. A stable concrete footing 300 mm deep is essential for any brick or stone retaining wall. In cold climates the base of the footing must lie below frost level to prevent movement of the ground as water freezes and thaws.

Plan the location of the wall and its trench carefully. Avoid excavating areas where there are underground cables or sewage pipes within 1.2 metres of the ground surface. If possible, locate the wall so that the soil excavated from the trench can be used to level or gently grade the ground behind the wall.

Anatomy of a brick retaining wall. Centred on a footing of solid concrete, this retaining wall rises 1 metre above the ground. The depth of the footing is 300 mm and extends 100 mm beyond the wall all round. The trench is 450 mm deep—the depth of the footing plus two brick courses.

The bricks are laid in alternate rows of headers (end-on bricks) and stretchers (side-on bricks) to form a solid wall two bricks thick. Weepholes built into the first row of bricks above ground level permit water to drain from the ground behind the wall; a filling of pea gravel behind the wall further assists drainage.

A coping of bricks laid on edge on top of the wall protects against penetration by rainwater, and a coating of bituminous paint on the back of the wall guards against dampness from the soil.

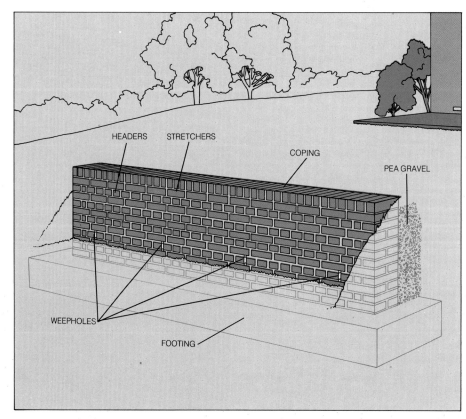

HEADERS STRETCHERS COPING PEA GRAVEL WEEPHOLES FOOTING

Building the Wall

1 **Excavating the site.** Working upwards from the base of the slope, cut away the earth where the proposed wall and its footing are to be built with a pick and spade. Dump the excavated soil behind the site of the wall where it will be used later to create a plateau, making the cut face slightly lower than the planned height of the wall. Tamp the apron of earth in front of the cut face.

2 **Digging the footing trench.** Starting 600 mm from the cut face, dig a trench at least 450 mm deep, and three times the width of the proposed wall. Check that the sides are vertical as you dig. Drive a stake into the bottom of the trench at one end so that its top will be level with the surface of the concrete. Drive in more stakes along the trench and use a spirit level and a straight piece of wood to make sure that the tops of the stakes are level *(right)*.

3 **Making the concrete footing.** In a wheelbarrow, mix batches of concrete made from a mix of 1 part Portland cement to 5 parts combined aggregate. Pour it into the trench, then tamp it flush with the top of the stakes *(right)*. Use a spirit level to check that the surface is even. Allow the concrete to dry for a minimum of 48 hours.

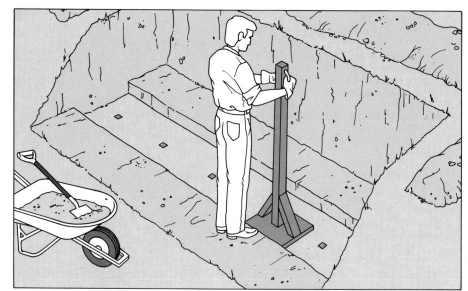

4 **Laying the bricks.** Establish a guideline for the first course of bricks by snapping a chalk line along the footing 100 mm from the front edge. Place a dry course of bricks along the inside of the line to establish the bonding pattern, using a piece of 10 mm dowelling to measure spaces between the bricks for the mortar joints. Begin mortaring the bricks in place; first build up the ends of the wall to a height of five courses, then fill in the courses between *(right)*. Use a spirit level to check that each end is vertical, and a guideline stretched between wooden or plastic blocks to ensure that each course is level and straight. Make weepholes *(inset)* in the first complete course of bricks above ground level by filling a vertical joint approximately every metre with sand instead of mortar. When the mortar is dry, brush the sand out of the weepholes.

GUIDELINE

WEEPHOLES

CHALK LINE

BLOCKS

5 **Completing the wall.** To cap the wall, lay the last course of bricks on edge *(right)*. Alternatively, use coping bricks *(inset, right)* or pre-cast concrete coping *(inset, left)*. Allow the mortar to dry for at least 10 days, then coat the back of the wall—the surface that faces the cut slope—with a waterproof bituminous paint.

WEEPHOLES

6 **Backfilling the wall.** Fill the cavity behind the wall with some of the excavated earth, leaving a space of about 300 mm immediately behind the wall. Fill this gap with pea gravel *(right)*, then top off the backfilled ground until it is level with the top of the wall. Level the earth in front of the wall, making sure the weepholes are not covered.

A Stone Wall for a Rustic Effect

1 **Laying the stones.** Following the procedures described on pages 29–30, prepare a concrete footing twice the thickness of the proposed wall. Starting at one end with a tie stone, lay the first course of stones 125 mm in from the edge of the footing on a 20 mm thick bed of mortar *(right)*. Outline the sides of the wall with regularly-shaped stones, and fill the centre with small, unevenly-shaped pieces; cover all the stones in each layer with mortar. As you build up the wall, "batter" the sides by insetting each course slightly from the last, using a slope gauge and spirit level to check the angle *(far right)*.

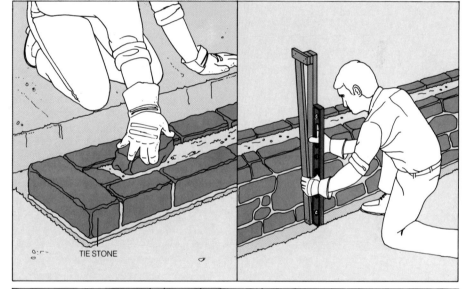

TIE STONE

2 **Completing the wall.** In the first course of stones clear of ground level, make weepholes by driving a broom handle into the wet mortar approximately every metre, pushing it right through to the other side of the wall. Cap the wall by mortaring a coping of flat stones over the last course of stones *(right)*. Allow the mortar to dry for at least 10 days, then waterproof the wall and backfill as shown in Step 6, above.

Last Step Before Planting: Preparing the Soil

Few experiences are as disheartening as watching the best parts of a newly planted landscape wither and die. Yet such a disaster is entirely preventable. When large groups of plants fail to flourish, the reason is likely to be either a failure to prepare the soil correctly or a failure to match the plants to the soil that has to sustain them.

All soil is composed of mineral particles of various sizes, ranging from fine, dense clay to coarse, loose sand; in addition, soil contains humus—a mixture of decayed vegetable matter and a small amount of animal matter—that acts as a fertilizer and is an important determining factor of the soil's texture. Good garden soil is spongy enough to retain moisture but porous enough for good drainage and air circulation *(page 26)*. It contains the nutrients which are essential for plant growth—nitrogen, phosphorus, potassium and other important trace elements. And it is neither too acid nor too alkaline—conditions that impair the ability of roots to extract nutrients from the soil.

The best soils—loams—contain sand, clay and humus in roughly equal parts. Few gardens are naturally favoured with such soil—but equally rare is soil so poor that it will destroy any plant put into it. And you can improve almost any soil by digging and incorporating soil conditioners and organic matter.

The first step in soil improvement is testing the physical structure and the chemistry of the existing soil. If you have had difficulty growing plants in your garden in the past, it may be worthwhile contacting the Department of Agriculture, or a local agricultural college, for advice on where soil samples can be analysed. But you can usually get all the information you need by performing a few simple tests yourself.

Begin by assessing the structure of your soil—that is, its proportions of clay, sand and humus. Soil with too much clay is dense and heavy, slippery when wet, hard and lumpy when dry. Because it retains water almost indefinitely, clay is a prime cause of drainage problems. Sandy soil, which is light and gritty, tends to dry too quickly, so that plants are parched and nutrients are leached out.

For a detailed picture of soil components, perform the water test shown opposite, Step 2; from it, you can accurately gauge the need for structure-improving conditioners. To break up clayey soil, use coarse builders' sand, available at builders' merchants and some garden centres. Ground gypsum (calcium sulphate), applied at the rate of 100 to 250 grams per square metre, can also be used to improve the texture of clayey soil. Both sandy and clayey soils should also be treated with organic matter, which makes sandy soils more spongy, clayey soils more porous. Moss peat, leaf mould and pulverized bark are the commonest conditioners of this kind. But the best soil conditioners, because they add nutrients as well as improve the structure of the soil, are well rotted manures, and compost—a rich, dark mixture of decayed vegetable matter that you can prepare yourself in your garden *(page 35)*.

To perform chemical tests, use an inexpensive soil-test kit, available at garden centres. The kit contains an array of test tubes and chemicals and a set of charts for interpreting the results of the test. Each of the chemicals responds to a specific soil characteristic—typically, the quantity of nitrogen, potassium or phosphorus, and the acidity or alkalinity of the soil, which is indicated by a pH number.

Neutral soil has a pH of 7, the midpoint in a pH scale that runs from 0 to 14. Above 7, soil is increasingly alkaline; below 7, it is increasingly acid. Most plants grow best in slightly acid soil, between 6.5 and 6.8 on the pH scale. Some popular plants, for example azaleas and rhododendrons, prefer a more acid soil; others, such as lilacs and delphiniums, thrive on mild alkalinity. A pH test, used in conjunction with the plant charts on pages 53, 59, 63, 82–83, 94–95 and 115 will help you to select the best plants to grow in your type of soil. But some soil conditioners are usually needed in addition, particularly in rainy, humid climates, which tend to produce excessively acid soil, and in very dry climates, which tend to produce alkaline soil.

To reduce acidity, add lime to the soil. A good dressing of lime (100 to 250 grams per square metre) should last about five years. For clay soils, it is best to use hydrated lime (calcium hydroxide); for sandy soil, ground limestone (calcium carbonate) will give a better performance—it is less soluble and will be leached away more slowly. Do not apply lime at the same time as manure—the chemical reaction between the two releases valuable nitrogen into the atmosphere—and be sure not to add lime to soil that will be used to grow lime-hating plants, such as azaleas and rhododendrons.

Alkaline soil can be corrected with magnesium sulphate (Epsom salts) or with iron sequestrols applied at the rate of 30 grams per square metre, or by adding farmyard manure, leaf mould or peat. Inorganic substances tend to be removed from the soil more quickly than organic conditioners, and should be applied every year.

The best time to test a soil and to improve its structure and pH rating is between four and six months before planting, to give the conditioners plenty of time to be thoroughly incorporated. Add organic matter and sand as you are digging the soil, then broadcast lime or magnesium sulphate on the surface, and rake it into the top few centimetres. Chemical fertilizers are usually added at planting time, so that rainwater does not leach them out of the soil before the plants can use them.

To dig a large area quickly and easily, use a power cultivator, available from plant hire companies. Your choice of cultivator depends largely upon your experience and special needs. A model with the engine mounted at the front and the tines set behind it is more stable and generally preferable for a beginner; a model with front-mounted tines is more manoeuvrable in tight places.

For a small area, manual digging may be a better choice; in fact, many professional landscapers consider manual digging preferable when preparing a garden bed, as opposed to a field for crops. The manual technique called double digging *(page 34)* is unfortunately the most arduous but also the most thorough method of preparing the soil. Because it ensures good soil to a depth of nearly 500 mm, it is ideal for a new flower bed, especially one intended for planting deep-rooted perennials.

Whatever method you choose, do not dig soggy soil, which breaks up into large, heavy clods that can dry as hard as rocks. To test for moisture, squeeze some soil in your hand; a sticky, compact mass that will not crumble is too wet. Three days after a fall of rain, when the soil is neither too wet nor annoyingly dusty and dry, is generally a good time to dig.

Analysing the Structure and Chemistry of Soil

1 Gathering samples. At several different spots within the area you intend to plant, dig holes about 150 mm wide and one spade (150 to 200 mm) deep. Slice a thin wedge of soil from the wall of each hole (*right*), deposit the soil in a plastic bucket and mix the samples together with the spade or a trowel. Be careful not to touch the soil samples with your hands.

Certain landscape features, particularly stone walls and foundations, shrubs and trees, can alter the pH of nearby soil. Test soil from each of these areas individually.

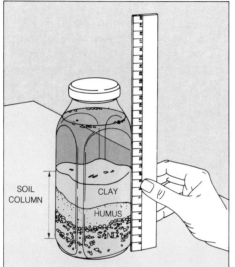

2 Analysing soil structure. Fill a litre bottle half full of water, then add soil until the bottle is nearly full. Cap the bottle and shake it vigorously to mix the soil and water together.

Wait for the soil to settle; this will usually take about three hours. Then, using a ruler held alongside the bottle, measure the height of the settled soil. In the same way measure the thickness of each layer: smooth, uniform clay at the top; darker topsoil and humus in the middle; sand and pebbles on the bottom. To determine the percentage of the soil represented by each component, divide each of these figures by the total height of the soil, and multiply by 100.

If your measurements show that the percentage of topsoil and organic matter is less than 25 per cent of the total, add moss peat, manure or compost. If the percentage of clay in the soil is greater than 25 per cent, plan to incorporate coarse sand or gypsum as well as humus when you are digging the ground (*page 34*). If the soil is more than 30 per cent sand, you will want to double the amount of added organic matter.

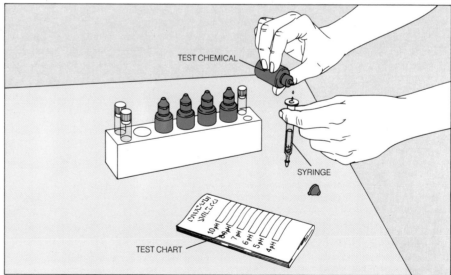

3 Using a chemical soil test kit. With a spoon, fill a syringe one-quarter full of soil, then add the amount of test chemical specified in the kit manual. Insert the plunger and shake it to mix the soil and the chemical thoroughly.

Filter the solution into a test tube by pushing the plunger. Compare the colour of the solution in the test tube with the colours on the appropriate test chart. In a chart for a test of chemical nutrients, each colour indicates the amount of a specific nutrient in the soil; in a pH test, colours represent pH levels. If the colour of the solution falls between two colours on a chart, estimate a pH number between the two levels.

Improving Soil with Air and Conditioners

Double digging. Outline the bed by driving a spade straight down into the earth with your foot, then cut parallel lines approximately 600 mm apart across the bed, marking off a series of rectangular digging sections. Dig out the soil from one of the end sections to the full depth of the spade (150 to 200 mm). Deposit the soil in a heap at the edge of the planting bed *(below, left)*.

Next, spread a 75 mm-thick layer of organic soil conditioner—either well-rotted manure or compost—in the bottom of the trench you have just made, then dig the conditioner into the 200 mm of soil below, using a fork, if necessary, to break up the soil. Then fill this trench with soil from the adjacent digging section *(below, right)*, leaving a second trench that is approximately 600 mm wide and 200 mm deep. Dig another 75 mm layer of organic soil conditioner into the soil that now fills the first section you dug up.

Spread conditioner in the trench of the second section, dig it in, and transfer the top 200 mm layer of soil from the third section to fill the second. Continue the process in this way until you reach the last section. Dig conditioner into the last trench, then fill it up with soil from the first section which you dumped at the edge of the planting bed, and again dig in conditioner.

Operating a power cultivator. Set the controls of the cultivator to neutral, position the machine at one corner of the planting bed, and set the tines to the correct depth for your soil—from 75 mm for heavy, clayey soil to 200 mm for sandy soil. Start the engine, then change into forward gear and guide the machine along one side of the bed. When you reach the far end of the bed, make a broad turn and work back in the opposite direction, creating a U-shaped area of dug soil; continue working back and forth in this way until you have moved across the entire bed *(inset)*. Then change into neutral, move the cultivator to the first undug strip and repeat the pattern until all the soil has been turned. For heavy soil, reset the tines at 150 mm and repeat the pattern.

For the second stage of cultivation, spread a 75 mm layer of soil conditioners such as coarse sand and humus over the earth. Set the tines at their maximum depth and work the conditioners into the soil. Use the same pattern as before, but work so that the second set of lines cross the first set at right angles.

If the cultivator jumps excessively, move it more slowly; if the problem persists, raise the tines slightly to cultivate at a shallower depth. You may have to experiment to find the right combination of speed and depth.

The Compost Heap: Free Fertilizer from Throwaways

Making a compost heap is rather like setting up a fertilizer factory in your back garden. The workers in the factory are millions of micro-organisms—the bacteria and fungi that cause all organic matter to decay. In compost, transformations that take years on a forest floor can occur in four to six months. More specifically, organic waste from garden and kitchen is converted into humus, which is rich in nutrients and capable of improving the structure of the soil as well.

Compost bins hold the material neatly and retain heat and moisture, which speed chemical changes. Such bins range from simple constructions of timber or wire to proprietary plastic bins in a range of sizes to suit all gardens. The simplest and easiest kind, shown below, is chicken wire—heavy-gauge mesh with rectangular openings about 150 by 100 mm—on an open circle of metal fencing stakes. Many gardeners build two bins: one for compost in the process of decaying, one for storing the finished product. Make each bin 1 to 1.5 metres high and at least 1.25 metres wide, with an opening wide enough for a wheelbarrow. If possible, place the bins in a shady area to retard drying, and keep a hose handy for watering the contents.

The ingredients of a compost heap are usually determined by what is readily available. A nearby riding stable, producing a constant and abundant supply of manure and rotted straw, is an obvious boon. Much more common ingredients of a compost heap are grass clippings and other garden refuse such as pulled weeds and hedge clippings, sawdust and wood shavings from a home workshop, wood ashes from a fireplace, torn-up newspapers, and organic waste from the kitchen such as vegetable scraps, crushed eggshells, coffee grounds and tea bags. Tree leaves can be added to a compost heap, but they are ideally used rotted down separately as leaf mould and returned to the soil to improve texture.

Although the variety of ingredients may be almost infinite, choosing the right amounts and mixing them together requires care. The micro-organisms in compost work best on a diet richer in carbon than in nitrogen; a ratio of 25 parts of carbon to 1 of nitrogen is ideal. To obtain or approximate this ratio, mix materials relatively high in one element with those relatively high in the other. Woody, coarse materials tend to be high in carbon: sawdust, for example, has a carbon to nitrogen ratio of 500 to 1, and leaves and straw range between 40 and 80 to 1. Green or soft materials—grass clippings, vegetable scraps, manure—have ratios between 15 and 20 to 1; compared with the ideal 25 to 1 ratio, such materials are high in nitrogen.

When you assemble the compost heap, work in alternate layers of natural materials and soil. Make thick layers of coarse natural materials (about 150 mm of crushed, fibrous stems, for example), thinner layers of light materials (about 75 mm of grass clippings, perhaps). A garden shredder, which can either be purchased or hired, reduces all composting materials to a single texture and speeds decomposition; if you use one, make all the layers 100 to 150 mm thick.

To provide nitrogen—essential food for the bacteria that break compost down—and to add valuable minerals, cover each of the layers of natural materials with a proprietary compost heap activator, or manure; then, if your soil is too acid, add lime. Wet each layer with a garden hose and seal it with 50 mm of soil. These soil sandwiches should be piled to the top of the bin; shape the topmost layer of soil to a dish-like form to help collect rainwater.

Most professional gardeners turn the pile with a fork every four weeks or so, a practice that speeds composting by incorporating air and by moving materials from the edges of the pile to the warm, brewing centre. Even in the coldest weather, the chemistry of a compost heap should generate perceptible heat; the poet Robert Frost described the process as "the slow, smokeless burning of decay".

When ready for harvest, a compost heap is reduced in bulk by at least a third, and its ingredients are uniformly dark and flaky. Use compost generously; a 50 mm layer mixed deep into your soil twice a year is an ideal tonic.

2 Building a Blanket of Green

Cover for a steep or rugged expanse. Sold by the tray, and easy to divide and plant with a trowel, pachysandra is one of the hardiest of the more common evergreen ground covers. Its deeply toothed leaves grow in clusters and form a lush carpet 200 to 250 mm high, ideal for terrain too steep or rocky for a traditional grass lawn.

For many home owners, landscaping begins and ends with the lawn. Certainly, more effort is expended in seeding, mowing, watering, fertilizing, weeding and patching lawns than in all other landscaping activities combined. A peculiar mystique associated with attractive lawns inspires this effort. Part of the mystique has to do with the lawn itself: a velvety expanse of green is undeniably beautiful and has become as much a status symbol as a two-car garage or an outdoor swimming pool. Part has to do with the relation of the lawn to other plantings: the most mundane arrangements of shrubs, trees and flower beds take on new dimensions when viewed against the rich green of a well-tended lawn.

Lawns were not always so precious. The word "lawn" is thought to be derived from a Celtic term for a glade-like open space between wooded areas. Centuries ago, these green spaces, sparsely covered with wild meadow grasses, were used as recreation areas where villages played the games that would later become bowling, tennis and croquet. At that time, the only plants in private gardens were those that could be used for food or for medicine.

Gradually, new species of hybrid grasses for home use evolved into today's wide assortment of durable, disease-resistant and uniformly toned lawn grasses. These breeds, nowadays often blended into mixes to suit different climates and types of use, make up the thick green blankets so many strive for and cherish, sometimes to the point of fencing in lawns and forbidding any traffic over them.

Actually, there is no need to pamper a properly maintained lawn. The correct mix of grass types should produce a lawn which is resilient enough to bounce back overnight from the pounding of children's games, or the occasional party. But there is no escape from a continuous regimen of lawn upkeep throughout the growing season. Mowing and watering have become weekend—and, often, weekday—institutions; fertilizing, aerating, scarifying, weeding and reseeding, though performed less often, are essential if you want to turn an ordinary lawn into an outstanding one.

One way to break free of the burden of grass care is to plant a lawn of chamomile or wild thyme. Sloping or uneven surfaces can be planted with leafy ground covers such as periwinkle or ivy: most of these plants require little more attention than periodic pruning, but they are comparatively fragile and, unlike grass, they cannot take the pounding of human activity and traffic. A number of ground covers are earth-bound climbers, many of which can be trained to grow vertically as readily as they do horizontally. This versatility can give an added dimension to a garden in which climbing and trailing plants not only cover the ground but extend the borders of the garden skywards in walls of green that mute or even blot out the lines and colours of unattractive structures.

Painstaking Care for a Perfect Lawn

A lush, deep-green lawn rewards the gardener who gives grass the special care it needs. But the reward does not come easily. Careful and painstaking mowing, fertilizing, watering and reseeding will help create a healthy lawn which should resist the invasion of weeds and pests.

Of these basic chores, mowing is by far the most time-consuming; in the spring, a close-mown lawn may need mowing every week. Ideally, grass should be mowed to about two-thirds of the height to which it has grown at mowing time.

For the best appearance of a lawn, cut a neat edge at the border. Most grasses can spread quickly into adjacent flower beds and unpaved paths. Although tools called edgers can stop their progress temporarily, you may want to consider a permanent solution—a so-called mowing strip, usually consisting of a concrete or brick border. The strip not only halts the spread of grass but eases mowing at the edge of the lawn by providing a grass-free path for the outer wheels of the mower.

In summer, when heat and lower rainfall slow grass growth, you will mow your lawn less but water it more. Like mowing, watering calls for some self-restraint (extreme over-watering can be as damaging as drought) and for careful timing. Frequent light waterings end up inhibiting root growth, because the grass need not root deeply in quest of ground water; an occasional thorough watering—perhaps once a week—is generally preferable. You can control the amount of water your lawn receives by using a sprinkler set for the correct intensity and area, and you should monitor the depth to which the water penetrates *(pages 42–43)*.

Grass does not, of course, live by water alone. To replace soil nutrients, fertilizers should be added to a lawn three times during the growing season. The timing depends on the type of grass, as indicated in the chart on page 53. For cold climate grasses, such as bent or fescue, make the first application in spring, the second and third within a month of each other in late summer and early autumn. Dry climate grasses should be fed twice in spring, with a month between applications, and then once again in midsummer.

Lawn fertilizers come in powder, pellet and liquid form, with labels that rate the nitrogen, phosphorus and potassium content according to a three-number code. One common rating, 10–6–4, indicates that 10 per cent of the fertilizer bulk is nitrogen, 6 per cent phosphorus and 4 per cent potassium. The higher the rating, the higher the dose of nutrients; a fertilizer with a rating of 20–12–8 contains twice as much nutrient as the same amount of 10–6–4.

Consider these differences in nutrient values when comparing fertilizer prices. An average lawn need 1.5 to 2 kilos of nitrogen per year for every 100 square metres. Therefore, the amount of fertilizer required for that area per year is between 15 and 20 kilos of 10–6–4, or from 7 to 10 kilos of doubly potent 20–12–8.

Most fertilizer formulations are balanced for normal feedings, with relatively large doses of nitrogen—roughly twice as much as either phosphorus or potassium. At least twice in each growing season, however, you should perform a soil test *(page 33)* to be sure that your soil is not deficient in any of these three minerals; if it is deficient in one of them, use fertilizer with a higher proportion of that mineral. As part of the soil test, measure the soil's pH, or acidity. Most grasses prefer a pH between 6 and 6.5; if necessary, adjust the pH with appropriate chemicals *(pages 32–33)*.

Patches of dead or damaged turf may be symptomatic of one of a number of common lawn problems *(pages 48–49)*. Even a lawn pampered by water and fertilizer can deteriorate with age. The ground beneath it may become so compacted by heavy traffic that grass roots cannot penetrate the hardened soil; at its worst, wear and tear can leave a lawn with bare patches, which must be reseeded *(page 45)*. Another common problem of ageing is thatch, a layer of dead grass and weeds that, if allowed to build up, can strangle new growth by preventing fresh seedlings from germinating.

Compaction and thatch are corrected with specialized lawn tools. An aerator *(pages 10–11 and 44–45)*, which extracts small plugs of earth to loosen compacted soil, may be needed for heavily used gardens or play areas as often as every two years. A layer of thatch more than 20 mm thick should be stripped off with a scarifier and removed immediately to allow new grass to grow *(page 45)*.

Safety Tips for Mowers

The blades of rotary lawn mowers are one of the major causes of accidents in the home. Whirling at speeds up to 300 kilometres per hour, such a blade can slice through a shoe or finger as easily as it cuts a blade of grass, and hurl stones and metal objects at high velocity. When using a rotary mower, therefore, you should always observe these precautions.

□ Before operating the mower for the first time, practise using the on-off controls, so that you know how to stop the machine quickly in an emergency.

□ Before each mowing, remove stones, branches, wires and rubbish from the lawn. Note and plan to avoid sprinkler heads and other fixed obstacles.

□ Unless your mower is equipped with a lever that enables you to adjust the height of the blade while the mower is running, make all cutting-height adjustments before starting the engine.

□ Before removing grass from the discharge chute of a power mower, always turn off the engine and wait until the blade has stopped turning.

□ When using a walk-behind mower on a hill, mow across the slope, not up and down it, to prevent your feet from slipping underneath the mower. Ride-on mowers, on the other hand, are much safer and more stable when they are run up and down a slope.

A Mower for Every Task

A cylinder mower. The scissoring action of reel blades against a fixed metal bed knife makes a smooth cut, particularly on thin grasses such as bent; cylinder mowers are less effective for trimming denser grasses such as rye grass. The blades need frequent sharpening and are easily damaged by twigs or pebbles. Manual models are more traditional, but the self-propelled power model shown here is preferable for larger lawns.

Rotary mowers. The sickle action of a high-speed rotary blade cuts a clean swathe through any type of grass, even in relatively irregular ground. Rotary blades for a walk-behind model (*below, right*) come in lengths from 450 to 600 mm; easily removable, the blade must be kept sharp with a steel file to avoid fraying or tearing the grass. For larger areas, a ride-on rotary mower (*below, left*) with a longer blade offers the advantages of speed and convenience.

BED KNIFE   REEL BLADES

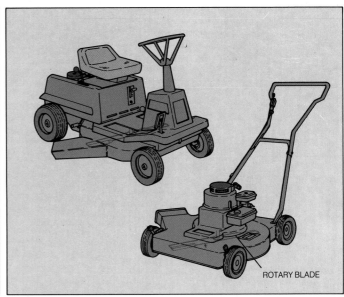

ROTARY BLADE

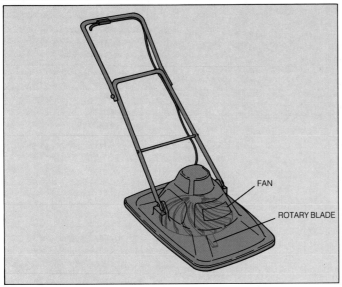

FAN

ROTARY BLADE

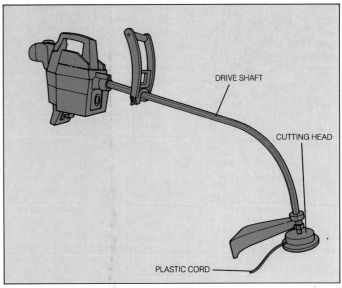

DRIVE SHAFT

CUTTING HEAD

PLASTIC CORD

An air cushion mower. A current of air produced by a rotating fan allows the mower to glide along about 6 mm above the ground, moving from side to side as well as backwards and forwards. The cutting action is similar to the rotary mowers shown above, but the lightness and flexibility of these machines make them ideal for sloping or irregularly-shaped lawns.

A weed trimmer. A plastic cord rotating at the end of a flexible drive shaft cuts through grass with a whipping action. The cutting head houses a reel of fresh cord, fed out by tapping the head against the ground. Originally designed to cut weeds, this trimmer is now commonly used for close, though uneven, mowing of grass around posts and other obstacles.

How to Mow a Lawn

Setting the blade height. With the engine off, tip the mower back and, reaching underneath it with a ruler, measure the distance from the blade to the bottom edge of the deck. Transfer this measurement to the outside of the deck with a pencil, then set the mower upright and measure from the mark to the ground to determine the present blade height.

If your mower is equipped with height-adjustment levers *(right)*, move the lever on each wheel to raise or lower the deck to the correct height—normally about 25 to 50 mm. On some models the height is adjusted by moving the wheel bolts to lower or higher holes. Ride-on mowers and some rotary models have a height lever that enables the operator to avoid obstacles by raising the blade while the mower is moving.

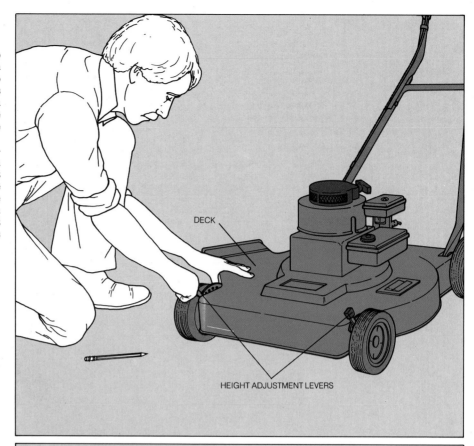

DECK

HEIGHT ADJUSTMENT LEVERS

Following the mowing patterns. On flat ground, start at the centre of the lawn and mow in a pattern of expanding rectangles, making gradual turns at each end of the lawn and overlapping each swathe by one-third the width of the mower. For a smooth, even finish, perform the next mowing at a 90-degree angle to this pattern; continue to alternate the direction of the cuts for each successive mowing. To achieve a neat pattern of stripes use a cylinder mower and mow in parallel lines across the lawn, lapping each cut by one-third the width of the mower *(inset)*.

When using a walk-behind mower on a slope, begin at the lowest edge, and mow across the slope in parallel lines up the hillside, lapping each cut as described above. With a ride-on mower, mow up and down the slope.

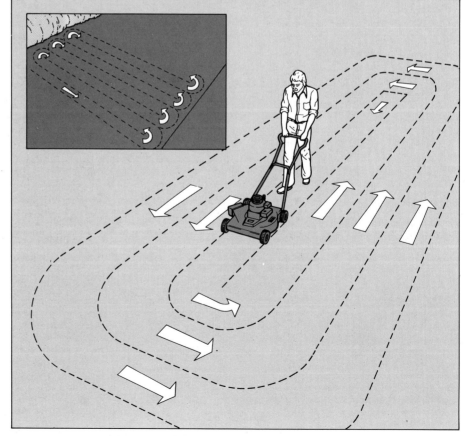

Trimming round obstacles. Use a weed trimmer to cut grass around posts or stones and underneath low-hanging branches or fencing, where a wheeled mower will not reach. Hold the cutting head parallel to the ground, 25 mm or so above the soil, and swing the head back and forth in smooth passes, working closer and closer to the obstacle until the level of the grass is the same as the surrounding turf.

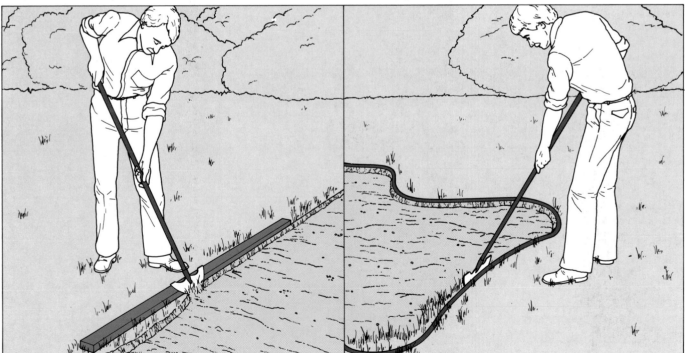

Edging. To cut a straight edge at the border of a path or flower bed, use a straight board as a guide for an edging knife. Hold the knife across the board at a slight angle and force the blade 50 to 75 mm into the earth along the board, slicing away about 25 mm of turf *(above, left)*. To produce a curved edge, lay a hose along the border and use it in the same way *(above, right)*, taking special care to keep the blade of the knife flat against the hose at all times.

Choosing the Right Sprinkler

In cool, wet regions, regular falls of rain make lawn watering superfluous, but most lawns need artificial soaking during extended dry periods. A lack of water soon makes itself apparent in changes of texture and colour. The grass loses its springy resilience and turns yellow. Eventually, the blades turn brown at the tips; soon afterwards, they may wither and die. Grass rescued early in the yellow stage by a thorough soaking from a sprinkler will revive in a few hours; brown blades may take weeks to re-establish themselves—or they may be beyond saving.

Each of the sprinklers shown on these pages is designed to water areas of a specific size and shape. Choose the sprinkler most suitable for your garden, then monitor its performance *(opposite page, below)* to avoid either wasting water or giving the grass insufficient water.

Almost all grasses send roots to a depth of at least 150 mm below the surface of the soil. Watering to a level below 150 mm, which encourages healthy root growth and vigorous turf, is best accomplished with a thorough soaking once a week rather than shallow sprinklings every day. But to a certain extent, the type of soil also governs watering practices. Water filters quickly through sandy soil, so that lighter but more frequent waterings will probably be needed. Dense, clay soils require a particularly slow, fine misting to allow time for water to seep in.

The best time of day for watering is the early morning; this soaks the ground soon enough to prevent the grass from wilting during the hottest part of the day. Watering in the evening can leave the blades damp and susceptible to fungus. Midday watering is worst of all—it is not only inefficient, because too much water evaporates, but it is also dangerous to the grass, because water on grass blades can focus the sun's rays and burn the plants.

An Array of Sprinkling Patterns

An oscillating sprinkler. Driven by water pressure from a garden hose, an oscillating sprinkler provides an even soaking of a rectangular area of grass. The curved crosspiece swings back and forth through all or part of the arc indicated by arrows; controls at the base of the crosspiece set the sprinkler to water all of the lawn, the centre alone or either half *(shaded areas, inset).*

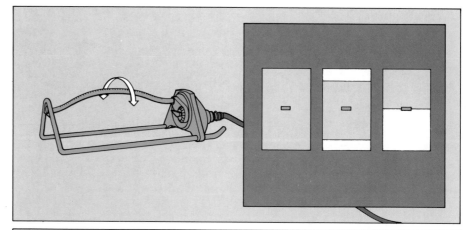

A turret sprinkler. Multiple turrets on the face of the sprinkler can be aimed to vary the length and width of a rectangular pattern of spray, from square to oblong *(inset).* As compared with an oscillator, a turret sprinkler provides a quick, heavy, somewhat uneven soaking.

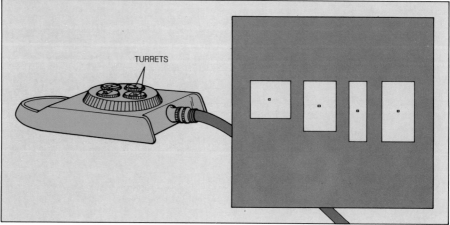

TURRETS

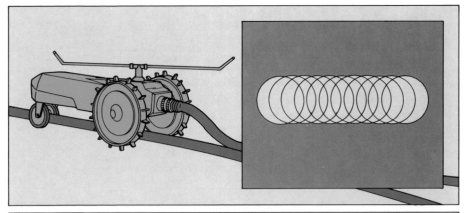

A travelling sprinkler. This self-propelled sprinkler is ideal for long, thin lawns. It follows the path of its own hose, even uphill, while the spinning nozzle soaks the grass in a spiral pattern *(inset)*. The travelling sprinkler shown here drags its hose behind it; other models reel in the slack hose as they move over the grass.

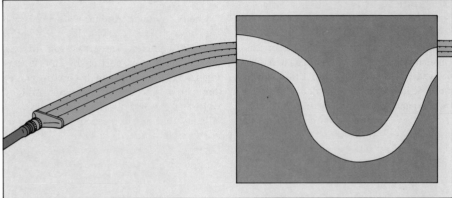

A perforated hose. Tiny holes along the top of a triple channel provide a fine soaking mist, excellent for clayey soils. The flexible hose can be laid to match the contours of an irregular plot *(inset)* or used with another hose section, linked by a Y-joint, to cover wider areas. Other models come with double or single channels; a one-channel hose, ideal for watering a border or a row of shrubs, is shown on page 86.

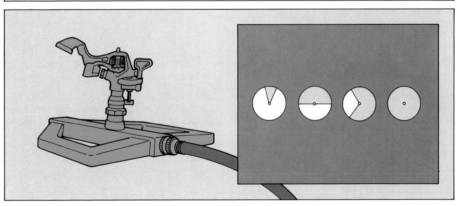

A pulsating sprinkler. The head of this sprinkler waters grass in a circular pattern that can be adjusted from a narrow wedge to a full circle *(inset)*. Constant side-to-side swings prevent water from pooling (each dose of moisture is absorbed by the grass before the nozzle delivers more) and the type of spray can be varied from a short, fine burst to a long, heavy jet.

A Test for Penetration

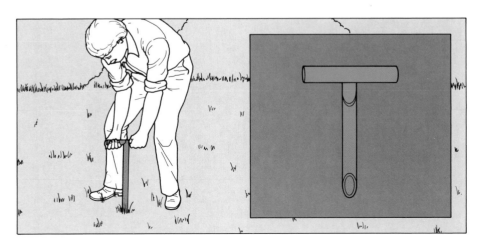

Boring with a core sampler. Soak the lawn for half an hour, then press and twist a core sampler—a hollow metal tube with a T-handle *(inset)*—into the soil to a depth of at least 200 mm. Withdraw the tool and inspect the bottom of the soil sample within it. If the soil is dark with moisture, the watering was adequate; fill the hole with the soil of the sample, topping it with the removed turf. If the soil is dry, refill the hole, water for another half hour and take another sample; repeat this procedure until a sample is moist at the bottom. Note the total time needed to saturate the ground to the correct depth, and soak the lawn this long in future waterings.

Techniques for a Healthy Lawn

Fertilizing with a trough spreader. Standing at a corner of the lawn, set the spreader gauge, which controls the rate at which fertilizer falls from the trough, according to the instructions on the fertilizer package. Open the trough with the release lever and start walking immediately at an even, moderate pace along one end of the lawn. Close the trough as soon as you reach the far side, in order to avoid burning the grass with excess fertilizer. Turn the spreader round, open the trough and run a second row of fertilizer alongside the first, positioning the spreader so that the two rows touch but do not overlap; a gap between rows will eventually leave dull streaks in the lawn. Run two similar rows at the opposite end of the lawn; then, running rows perpendicular to the end rows, fill in the remaining area *(inset)*.

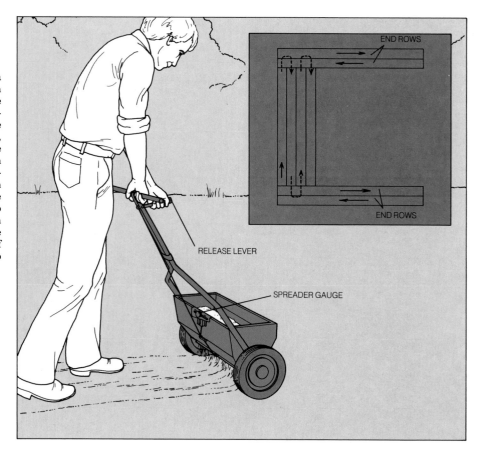

END ROWS

END ROWS

RELEASE LEVER

SPREADER GAUGE

Breaking up compacted soil. Saturate the ground with a sprinkler a day in advance. Then, for a small lawn, thrust a hollow tine aerator *(below, left)* into the ground at 150 mm intervals, driving it to a depth of 50 mm in sandy soil, and 100 mm in clay soil. Start by working along one boundary, and then back and forth parallel to this line, raking up the extracted cores as you go. If the soil has become so compacted that it is not possible to drive the aerator to the correct depth, make a shallower pass with the aerator, resoak the lawn and try again.

For large areas, use a self-propelled power aerator *(below, right)*, which can be hired from a tool rental shop. Roll the machine into position on the lawn, pull the starter cord and warm the engine with the clutch disengaged for three minutes. Release the clutch to set the tines in motion, then adjust the throttle to maintain a slow, even speed. Guide the aerator in the pattern used for mowing *(page 40)*, but do not overlap the rows.

Scarifying. For a small plot of grass, use a scarifier *(right)*. Holding the rake handle at a 30-degree angle to the ground, drag the rake across the lawn in parallel lines, exerting enough downward pressure to drive the teeth about 12 mm into the soil; take care to avoid uprooting the grass or loosening the turf. Remove the loosened material with a springtine rake and mow the lawn to sever any sprigs raised by the rake.

Reseeding a Bare Patch

1 **Preparing the soil.** Turn the soil in the plot with a fork, digging down about 150 mm. Remove 75 mm of soil and work the remaining soil to break up clods. Dust the area lightly with lawn fertilizer and add a 75 mm layer of moss peat, then mix together the soil, fertilizer and peat thoroughly with the fork.

Make the soil even with the surrounding earth by tamping it down with your foot. Your footprint should be no more than 10 mm deep in the soil mix; if necessary, adjust the soil level, either by removing mix or by adding more and tamping it down. Rake over the surface to smooth it.

2 **Reseeding.** Sprinkle seeds of grass about 3 mm apart over the patch, dropping the seeds from between your thumb and forefinger to avoid over-seeding. Using a rake, work the seeds into the top 3 mm of soil mix, then tamp the soil lightly with the back of a spade. Spray the soil with a light mist from a garden hose or watering can.

Fighting Weeds by Hand and Herbicide

The best defence against an invasion of lawn weeds is the lawn itself. A dense carpet of healthy turf can prevent weeds from gaining a toehold, by depriving them of the sunlight they need to germinate and multiply. But even in the best-kept lawn, some weeds are inevitable. When they do arise, they must be removed with a weeding fork or killed by chemicals.

Botanists distinguish between grassy and broad-leaved weeds, and the two types call for different chemical treatments. Grassy weeds can be caught early with a pre-emergent weedkiller, which destroys the germinating plants just as they are emerging; established weeds have to be treated with a post-emergent type, which attacks the growing plant.

Selective weedkillers attack susceptible broad-leaved weeds such as dandelion and plantain but do not kill lawn grasses. They are best applied as mixtures—such as 2,4.D and Dicamba—in spring or early summer when weeds are growing and the soil is moist. Do not mow the grass immediately before selective weedkiller treatment as it reduces the weed's intake area.

Chemical weedkillers must be used with caution: they can be harmful to animals and humans; they can attack trees and shrubs that are accidentally treated; and the grassy-weed chemicals also present a hazard to some turf grasses. Check the package label to be sure that the one you choose is safe for the grasses in your lawn, particularly if it is freshly sown.

To protect yourself and nearby plants, spray only on windless days; always wear rubber gloves and wash your hands immediately after use. Your best protection, however, is to reduce the use of chemicals by stopping a weed invasion before it spreads. The spot treatments shown on this page, applied in spring before weeds have established a toehold, can eliminate the need for broader coverage later on.

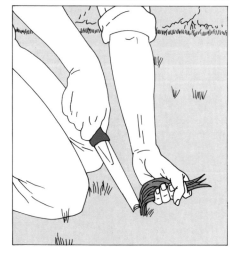

Spot Treatments That Catch Weeds Early

An aerosol herbicide. Hold the aerosol can 200 to 300 mm above the weed, and spray a one-second burst on to the centre of the plant, coating the leaves and main stem. Allow the weed about two weeks to shrivel and die, then remove it and re-seed *(page 45)* or sprig *(page 51)* the bare spot.

A brush-on weedkiller gel. Using the brush in the lid of the gel pot, paint as large an area of weed leaf as possible. The gel needs about six hours of dry weather to be fully absorbed. After two to four weeks, when the treatment has taken effect, remove the weed and reseed the bare patch.

A weeding fork. Grasp all the weed's runners or leaves in one hand; with the other, drive a weeding fork 75 or 100 mm into the earth alongside the main root. Levering the fork back and forth in the surrounding soil to work the roots free, pull up lightly on the bunched leaves until you can remove the weed with all its roots intact. It may be necessary to dig the fork all the way round a very stubborn weed; you must remove the weed without tearing its leaves or breaking its roots.

Treating a Large Area

Using a pressurized sprayer. Along one end of the weed-infested area, mark off a 1-metre strip with a pair of staked parallel strings. Build up pressure in the sprayer with a few strokes of the hand-pump, then spray the area between the strings, holding the spray tube about 300 mm above the grass and moving it quickly and steadily for a light, even coverage. Next, move one of the strings to mark off an adjoining strip, and treat this strip in the same way. Repeat this procedure until you have sprayed the entire area.

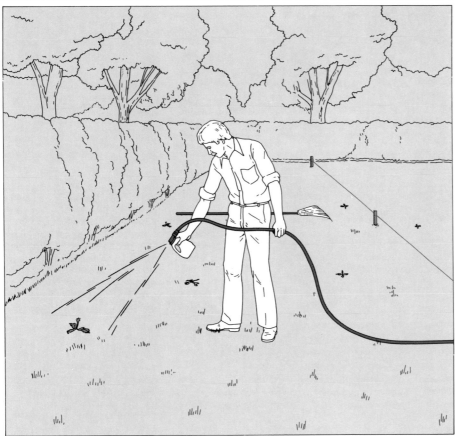

Using a garden-hose sprayer. With string and stakes, mark off a 20 square-metre area; set a conspicuous marker, such as a grass rake, in the middle of the area. Fill the reservoir with weedkiller or with the mixture of weedkiller and water specified in the label instructions; then screw the sprayer head on to a garden hose and attach the reservoir to the sprayer head. Open the hose valve and start the sprayer by covering the air-siphon hole or by depressing the trigger lever, depending on your model. Spray the area with a light, even coat, adjusting your movement and the force of the spray so that the reservoir is half empty when you reach the half-way marker.

Common Lawn Problems: Symptoms and Cures

Patches of dead or dying grass are a sure sign of lawn trouble, but isolating the cause of the problem is not always a simple matter. Damage to a lawn can stem from various sources: inadequate care, unsuitable growing conditions, pests or other external factors. These charts show how to cure a number of miscellaneous injuries, and how to deal with common lawn pests.

The best defence against any of these problems is a healthy lawn. If the tasks on pages 38–47 are carried out effectively the lawn will be better able to resist damage and pests than a neglected lawn.

With all chemical treatments, follow the

Common Lawn Problems

Problems	Symptoms	Controls
Algae, Green Scum	A green or blackish scum, which cracks and peels back when dry, may form in low, wet or shaded areas, especially if soil is compacted.	Improve drainage and aerate soil to relieve compaction *(page 44)*. Apply copper sulphate, diluted in water to the strength recommended by the manufacturer, or mercurized lawn sand at 125 g per square metre.
Buried Debris	Patches of grass turn pale green and dry out because root growth is inhibited by buried scraps of left-over timber, plaster or metal.	Dig out debris; if necessary, replace soil and reseed or lay turf.
Compacted Soil	Lawns develop hard, bare spots or areas of knotgrass.	Use a power aerator on large areas or dig up smaller spots to a depth of 125 to 150 mm, incorporating moss peat and fertilizer, or reseed or returf in autumn. If the section is one that must be walked on frequently, try a rye grass seed mix, or replace the grass with paving.
Dog Urine	Dead areas in the lawn, roughly circular, show a rich green circumference.	Dig and reseed as above. To prevent further dead areas, water copiously to dilute and disperse urine when seen to occur.
Earthworms	Small mounds of earth appear on the surface of the lawn, discolouring the grass and inhibiting growth.	Reduce worm fertility by always removing grass clippings before they decay. Apply sulphate of ammonia or sulphate of iron to the affected area, and top dress with peat. Chlordane, applied in autumn, gives longer-term control.
Fertilizer Burn	Grass browns, especially in hot weather, because inorganic fertilizers have been spread unevenly and/or too heavily and not watered in.	Always water lawns thoroughly after applying inorganic fertilizers. If damage occurs, drench the lawn, especially in injured areas, to leach excess fertilizer deep into the soil and away from the grass roots. Avoid using inorganic fertilizers during hot weather.

Controlling Pests That Attack Lawns

Pests	Description	Signs of Infestation
Ants	These insects can be troublesome to lawns if they are present in large numbers. They can be either black or red and are about 6 mm or less in length.	In sandy soils, ants often build small mounds of earth around the entrance to their nests, making the lawn surface unsightly and smothering the grass beneath.
Chafer Grubs	The plump, white curled larvae of garden chafer beetles grow to about 12 mm in length and feed near the surface on grass roots. Adult beetles emerge in early summer.	In spring and autumn, grubs eat away at the grass roots, creating brownish dead patches that are slightly soggy and can be lifted out of the lawn.
Leather Jackets	Leather jackets are the larvae of the long-legged flies known as crane flies or daddy longlegs. The brown or grey grubs originate as eggs laid by the female fly in late summer.	Grubs feed on grass roots near the soil surface, creating patches of brown in early spring. They are particularly troublesome after a wet autumn.

manufacturer's instructions scrupulously; always mix and apply in the specified amounts, and take heed of warnings about harmful effects. Many garden chemicals can be a hazard to humans, birds, household pets and beneficial insects such as bees. Avoid spraying or dusting on a windy day, do not smoke when using insecticides, and never spray or dust around food.

Always dispose of left-over chemicals carefully, not where children or pets may find them. Wash any equipment thoroughly after use and do not use sprayers for any other purpose. Store all chemicals in a safe place, preferably in a locked cupboard.

Problems	Symptoms	Controls
Incorrect Mowing	Lawns cut too closely weaken, turn yellowish and often look diseased. Cutting with a dull mower frays leaf tips, which then turn brown.	Set mower to the recommended height for your type of grass. Mow often enough so that you remove no more than one-third of the grass height at one time. Keep mower blades sharp.
Incorrect Watering	Light sprinkling encourages shallow roots and weakened, stunted grass; overwatering encourages lawn diseases.	Water only during dry spells, when the grass begins to wilt, soaking the soil to a depth of at least 150 mm. Water early in the day so that the grass will dry before nightfall; grass that remains damp overnight is especially susceptible to fungus diseases.
Peltigera Canina (Lichen)	Grey-brown leafy growths form in damp, shaded areas, discolouring the grass.	Improve drainage, where necessary, and aerate the soil to prevent further lichen growth. Rake out the lichen. Apply compound fertilizer and mercurized lawn sand at 125 g per square metre or a mixture of 125 g sand and 15 g sulphate of iron per square metre.
Moles	Long, rounded ridges, soft when stepped on, indicate mole tunnels close to the surface of the ground.	Mole baits and mole traps are usually effective. Since moles eat grubs, make sure you control grubs with proper chemicals (*below*). Smoke pellets are more effective in heavier, wet soils than in dry, sandy soils.
Moss	Moss may grow in patches or take over entire areas of lawn. It thrives in shady, moist conditions and in acid or compacted soil.	In early spring when the soil is moist, treat with lawn sand. Improve the drainage, remove thatch, correct soil acidity and feed with fertilizer.
Thatch	An accumulation of mowed grass stems and dead or dying roots that block water, air and nutrients. It leaves lawns dry and ailing.	Use a scarifier, as shown on page 45, in early autumn.

Chemical Controls	Other Control Methods
Apply chlordane, BHC or carbaryl. Or a slow-acting liquid killer containing trichlorphon can be placed near the nest; the ants will carry it back to their queen.	Scatter ant hills with a brush before mowing the lawn.
Apply BHC dust or spray, or chlordane according to manufacturer's instructions in spring or early autumn.	Roll the lawn in autumn or late spring in order to crush the grubs or adults.
Apply BHC dust or spray; this is most effective in autumn, at the early stages of the grubs' development.	Soak the area with water, then cover with black polythene or tarpaulin overnight. The moisture will induce the grubs to the surface. Improve drainage.

Three Foolproof Ways to Start a New Lawn

To establish a lawn on an empty plot or to renovate an old lawn terminally choked with weeds, you must build a lawn from scratch. The job is not complicated, but it does involve heavy preliminary work. Before planting can begin, the area must be cleared. The ground must be cultivated to a depth of about 150 mm. Then, depending on the results of soil tests, it may have to be further improved with fertilizers and conditioners *(pages 32–35)*. Finally, the plot must be raked and rolled smooth. Then the soil is ready to support a new lawn.

The type of grass you should choose for your plot depends largely upon the climate of your region. No turf grass is suitable everywhere; many will not survive extremes of heat or cold, and some tolerate dry climates better than others do. But certain rules of thumb apply. Cool-climate grasses, for example bents and fescues, are well adapted for temperate climates. Such grasses grow slightly in spring, more slowly in the warm months of a relatively short summer and thrive in a cool, wet autumn. Ideally, they should be planted in late summer to take advantage of the autumn growing season, but they can also be sown in spring after the last frost.

Warm-climate grasses, such as zoysia, Bermuda or Buffalo grass, have the opposite schedule, flourishing in the heat of a long summer and growing very slowly in the winter months. These are planted in warm regions in spring or early summer, when daytime temperatures are regularly above 20°C. For lawns with a combination of sunny and shaded areas or in climates with wide variations of temperature, a mixture of several grasses gives the best results. Mixtures are sold with the percentage of each grass type on the package, so you can choose the mix that best suits your conditions of light and climate.

With the soil bed prepared and the grass type chosen, you have a choice of three ways to plant the lawn, based on seed, sprigs or turf. Direct seeding is the least expensive method but also the slowest. Sprigs, which are more commonly used in warm climates, consist of grass stems with roots and blades attached. Turfing, in which rectangular pieces of live turf are set on bare ground, is the quickest of the three methods—and the most expensive.

If you choose to seed a lawn, follow the seeding density given on the label of the grass mixture—a typical rate would be 20 or 30 grams of seed per square metre—and spread the seed evenly over the area by hand or with a mechanical spreader. Do not try to speed growth by using more than the recommended quantity of seed; the seedlings will essentially rob one another of nutrients and will eventually produce an unhealthy-looking lawn. Once they are in the ground, seeds require constant moisture to germinate; in a hot climate, water the lawn daily, or even every few hours in extreme heat. In a temperate climate water the seeds every few days during dry weather. Leave the grass untouched until it is 75 mm high, then mow it to promote vigorous, dense growth.

Most warm climate grasses are planted by sprigging. Coverage is slow because the seedlings must send out new shoots to fill the gaps left between them in planting; but in the meantime the new lawn is somewhat less fragile than a lawn grown from seed. Sprigs are set into shallow furrows scratched into the earth with a hoe blade.

For those who want the instant gratification of a ready-made, almost prefabricated lawn, turfing is ideal. Suppliers will be able to advise on the correct turf for heavy or light wear. Mats of turf are ready for use immediately, but laying them down calls for careful levelling of the bed and much heavy lifting of the rolls. You will get the best results if you lay the turf within 36 hours after delivery, while it is still fresh and moist. Do not lay turf in summer when there is a risk of dry weather. Level the plot before the delivery date; keep the soil bed moist but not muddy while laying the rolls, to ensure good contact with the soil—and, obviously, do not order more turf than you can lay within 36 hours.

A New Lawn from Seed

1 Firming the soil. After digging and conditioning the soil, push a lawn roller, empty of water, over the entire area. Roll the area first in parallel strips, then go over it again at a right angle *(inset)*. If necessary, continue to firm and compact the soil until your feet barely leave an indentation; if the soil remains soft, fill the roller half full of water to add weight.

Smooth and spread the soil with a rake. Hold the rake at a 20 to 30-degree angle so that you avoid gouging the soil, and work the tines back and forth across the surface, pulling out and discarding any stones, rubbish or weeds. Finally, roll the soil once again to firm the surface. Do not firm the soil after heavy rain.

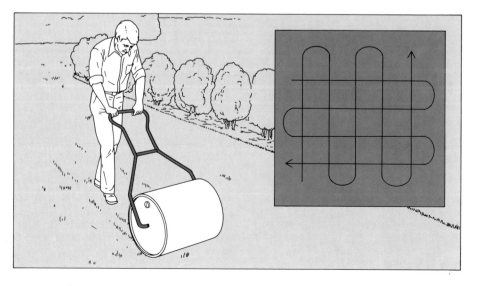

2 Smoothing the bed. Weight a ladder with a heavy plank and a pair of concrete blocks, tie the ends of a rope to one of the uprights and drag the ladder over the soil to slice off protruding mounds and fill depressions. Every 3 metres, set a spirit level across the ladder to check the slope of the bed; it should run slightly downwards from the house, so that it will channel water away from the foundation walls. If necessary, regrade the bed (pages 24–25) to adjust the slope. Finally, use a rake to roughen the soil lightly to a depth of 10 mm.

3 Sowing seed by hand. Measure out the correct quantity of seed for the entire area according to the supplier's instructions and divide it into two equal portions. Walk slowly over the plot in parallel lines, scattering seed from your open fist in 1.5 metre arcs until you have sown half the seed; sow the entire area again with the other half of the seed, walking in rows at right angles to the first direction. Rake the area once to a depth of 3 mm with a springtine rake to mix the seed into the soil, and soak it with a fine mist.

Planting with Sprigs

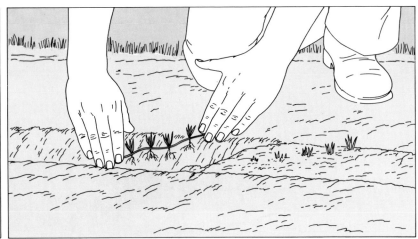

1 Furrowing the soil. After preparing and levelling the soil (Steps 1 and 2), soak the bed with water. Let the water seep in for 24 hours; then, with the corner of a hoe blade, cut a series of straight furrows 75 to 100 mm deep and 150 to 300 mm apart. Rows of sprigs planted 150 mm apart usually form a full lawn in three to six months; rows set 300 mm apart take twice as long.

2 Setting the sprigs. At 150 to 300 mm intervals, place the sprigs in the furrows, slanting them upwards from the bottom of a furrow to the top of one side. Pack soil gently round the roots with your hands, leaving some blades of each sprig protruding above the ground. Smooth the soil and level it round the sprigs. When you have planted all of the sprigs, soak the area with a fine mist; water frequently during periods of dry weather.

An Instant Lawn
from Rolls of Turf

1 **Laying the turf.** After preparing the bed *(pages 50–51, Steps 1 and 2)*, roughen the surface slightly with a rake and wet the soil thoroughly. Unroll the turf gently to avoid breaking off corners and edges, and lay the first course as flat as possible along a straight path or a staked string to provide a straight edge. For later courses, kneel on a piece of wooden board or planking laid across the new turf, to avoid creating depressions and raising the edges of sections. Butt the turf rolls as tightly as possible against each other, staggering the ends in an ordinary bricklaying pattern. If a laid roll feels uneven, roll it up and re-level the ground beneath it. Finally, fill any gaps between sections, cutting small pieces from a spare roll with a sharp knife or the edge of a trowel.

2 **Establishing root contact.** Standing on a piece of planking, tamp the turf with a tamping tool or with a board and rubber mallet, pressing the turf firmly against the soil bed; alternatively, roll the turf with an empty lawn roller *(page 50)*. If, by either method, you inadvertently lift the edge of a turf section, carefully tamp it down.

If the weather is dry, water the turf every few days until it roots in the soil. To determine whether the turf has rooted, try to lift a small piece by the grass blades; if the turf has taken root, the blades will tear.

Choosing Grass for Your Lawn

Grass type	Recommended soil type and pH	Planting method	Speed of growth	Texture	Wear tolerance	Shade tolerance	Characteristics and maintenance
Cool-climate							
Agrostis stolonifera (creeping bent)	Fertile soils 5.5 to 7.5	Seed Sprig Turf	Slow	Fine	Poor	Poor	A thickly growing, fine-leaved, shiny green grass for close, well-maintained and lightly used lawns; scarify in spring.
Agrostis tenuis (common bent)	Fertile soils and poor, dry soils 3 to 7.5	Seed Turf	Slow	Fine	Very poor	Very poor	As above.
Festuca rubra ssp. commutata (chewing's fescue)	All fertile soils except heavy clays 4 to 8	Seed Turf	Medium	Fine	Poor	Moderate	For fine lawns and low maintenance mixes and for flower meadows.
Festuca rubra ssp. rubra (creeping red fescue)	Best on sandy soils 5.5 to 7.5	Seed Turf	Medium	Fine	Poor	Moderate	A fine grass for lightly used lawns.
Lolium perenne (perennial rye grass)	All fertile, drought-free soils 5.5 to 8	Seed Turf	Very fast	Coarse	Very good	Poor	A thickly growing, broad-leaved grass for hard-wearing lawns and sports fields; requires frequent cutting, though there are dwarf varieties which reduce this need.
Phleum bertolonii (lesser Timothy)	Heavy soils 5 to 8	Seed Turf	Fast	Coarse	Moderate	Moderate	A fine-leaved grass for hard-wearing lawns on heavy clays.
Poa pratensis (smooth-stalked meadow grass, Kentucky bluegrass)	Light, fertile soils 3 to 8	Seed Turf	Very slow	Medium	Good	Good	Dense, rich-green, fine-textured turf. Drought-resistant and semi-dormant in warm weather.
Warm-climate							
Buchloë dactyloides (Buffalo grass)	6 to 8.5	Seed Turf	Slow	Medium	Good	Good	A thickly growing, broad-leaved grass; susceptible to frost. Requires watering in dry season; scarify in spring.
Cynodon dactylon (Bermuda grass)	Fertile and infertile (incl. salty) soils 5.5 to 7	Seed Sprig Turf	Fast	Fine	Very good	Poor	Dense, lush grass; good for heavy wear, drought and frost tolerant; scarify in spring.
Pennisetum clandestinum (Kikuyu grass)	Sandy to sandy loams, slightly acid to neutral 6 to 6.5	Seed Sprig Turf	Fast	Coarse	Very good	Poor	Dense, coarse grass for heavy wear; deep roots make it very drought tolerant. Scarify in spring. Can be pernicious weed in borders.
Zoysia matrella (Manila grass)	Fertile, sandy loams 5.5 to 7.0	Sprig Turf	Very slow	Fine	Very good	Good	Dense greyish to moss green turf; susceptible to frost. May be left unmown to form a ground cover 200 to 250 mm high. Needs constant watering and fertilizing.

Common grass types. Use this chart to help select grasses suitable for your climate and soil type, and for the intended use of your lawn. Grasses are divided into cool-climate types, suitable for temperate climates with year-round rainfall, and warm-climate types suitable for dry climates with rainfall concentrated in either summer or winter. Each type is listed by its Latin botanical name in alphabetical order, followed by its common English name. Across the top, the column headings define the soil type and pH requirements *(pages 32–33)* of each species, the variety of different planting methods, the growing speed, the texture, and tolerance to wear and shade of the lawn which is eventually produced. The column on the far right describes the characteristics and maintenance needs of each species.

Grass seed and turf are sold in mixes of species, chosen to suit the growing conditions and the use to which the lawn will be put. Sprigs are more commonly planted as a single species.

Weaving Diversified Carpets of Ground Covers

The low, rambling plants called ground covers, which grow in thick beds or mats, offer attractive alternatives to grasses in a variety of situations. On hillsides, ground covers check soil erosion and eliminate the troublesome—and risky—job of mowing on a slope. Many flourish in the shade and make hardy plantings for sunless areas that might otherwise be empty of greenery. And their diversity of colour, foliage and flowers provides decorative notes that are ideal for breaking up the monotony of open spaces or forming a transition between low grasses and tall shrubs.

Literally hundreds of plants can be used as ground covers. They range in size from dainty, 75 mm baby's tears to spindly, 600 mm-tall Scotch heather, and in colour from the deep green of Irish ivy to the bright yellow flowers of St. John's-wort. The evergreens, such as bearberry and juniper, keep a garden verdant all year long; deciduous plants, such as lily of the valley and sweet woodruff die back in winter. Some herbaceous ground covers, such as thyme, are prized for their fragrance. And certain fast-growing climbers—Virginia creeper for example—can be trained to flourish flat on the ground.

Choosing ground covers is not a matter of taste alone. The chart on page 59 lists some of the popular varieties and provides information on their special requirements of soil and climate; in addition, you should consult your nursery about the varieties that are most appropriate for your area. Before purchasing the plants, calculate exactly how many you will need: as a general rule, two to three such plants will cover a 30 by 30 cm area of soil.

Some ground covers, such as evergreen candytuft and sandwort, can be grown from seed. More commonly, however, they are sold as immature plants; they come either assembled in groups and planted in a rooting medium in a shallow, plastic tray as in the illustration below, or planted individually in small pots.

To help keep weeds at bay, mulch the ground with a layer of pulverized bark before you begin transferring the immature plants from their containers to the ground. (Even with such protection, the ground covers will have to be weeded—as often as every few days during the first year or so.) The mulch should be spread before planting because it is much easier and safer to dig holes in the ground through mulch than it is to distribute the bark around the delicate young plants.

Once the plants are out of their containers, plant them as quickly as possible so that their roots will not dry out. Experienced gardeners use an economical three-step trowelling technique (*opposite page, above*) to get the plants into the ground in the least amount of time. In dry climates, the young plants will need a great deal of water—a thorough drenching with a garden hose set for a fine mist, every other day for the first month.

After they have become well established, ground covers may run rampant. If they are not kept in check with judicious pruning, they will start to encroach on lawns and take over adjacent flower beds. Such vigorous growth, however, represents an opportunity for the gardener as well as a disadvantage. You can very easily propagate new plants either by dividing or taking cuttings from already established ground covers (*pages 56–57*).

Growing new ground-cover beds from old has advantages other than that of helping to control unwanted sprawl. It is much less expensive than buying extra plants from a nursery and it also ensures a uniformity of appearance from one bed to another. New plants can never exactly match established ones in colour or shape, but plants that are grown by division or cutting will display characteristics identical to those of the parent plants.

Getting Tiny Plants Off to a Good Start

1 **Separating the plants.** Work both hands under the rooting medium and lift the entire rectangle of packed medium out of the tray in one piece. Then separate the plants with your fingers, taking care not to injure the roots.

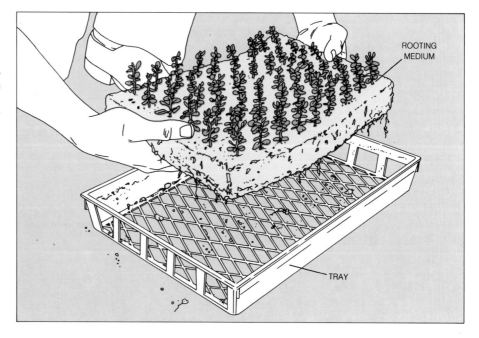

ROOTING MEDIUM

TRAY

2 **Setting the plants.** Working quickly, set the plants into the soil by a three-step procedure. First, prepare a planting hole: push a trowel down through the mulch and into the soil, then pull the trowel towards you, cutting a pocket in the ground *(below, left)*. Secondly, put the plant in place: holding the soil back with the trowel, set a plant in the pocket, with about 5 mm of its stem below ground level *(below, centre)*. Finally, use the trowel to push the displaced soil back into the pocket *(below, right)*, taking care not to dislodge or bruise the plant.

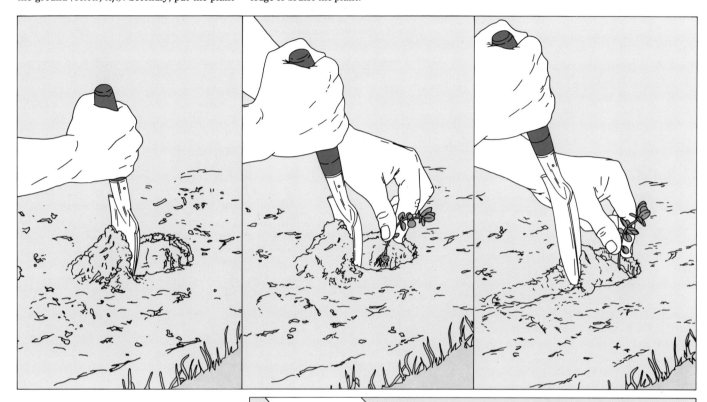

3 **Tamping down the soil.** Smooth out the soil and mulch with your fingers, patting the mulch down round the stem to form a slight depression that will catch and hold moisture *(inset)*. Set in the remaining plants, and water them for at least half an hour with a sprinkler or with a hose set for a fine mist. In dry climates, continue to water the new plants every other day for a month.

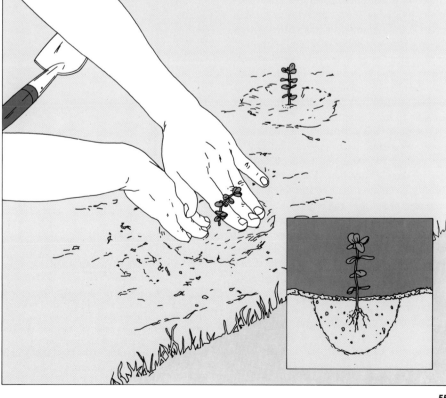

Multiplying by Dividing or Cutting

Ground covers can be propagated by three different methods: layering, cutting and division. Layering, the method in which a branch is made to root in the soil without being cut from the parent plant, is used more commonly for shrubs than for ground covers. However, some woody ground covers, such as winter creeper, respond very well to layering; if you choose this method for an appropriate plant, follow the instructions given on page 93.

In propagation by cutting, a piece is removed from the upper part of a well-established plant at least a year old, and placed in a spot where it can sprout roots of its own. Plants with succulent, non-woody stems, such as bearberry and periwinkle, grow well from cuttings.

Ideal parent plants for cuttings have crisp stems that snap off cleanly when bent sharply. Each cutting should contain three to five nodes—small bumps along the stems, making locations where new roots will emerge. In order to encourage rapid and healthy root growth, the stems are dipped in a synthetic, powdered plant hormone, available from nurseries or garden centres, then planted in trays filled with a rooting medium such as a combination of sand and moss peat in equal proportions. When covered with sheets of glass or plastic, the trays become miniature greenhouses, protecting young plants until they are able to survive outdoors.

Ground covers with thick root masses—sweet woodruff, pachysandra and lily of the valley, for example—respond best to the method of division. Large clumps of established plants, each containing a dozen or more stems, are uprooted, and the individual rooted stems are then separated and planted somewhere else. Plants which have been propagated in this way do not require such close attention as cuttings, but they have one requirement in common: like newly purchased plants, both must be watered regularly.

The time of year to propagate new plants depends partly on the type of plant, partly on climate. Check with the nursery that supplied the original plants to find out the best time for your plants and locality.

Propagation by Cutting

1 **Obtaining a cutting.** Remove a 75 to 150 mm length from a parent plant stem then cut through the removed stem with a sharp knife, making a clean, sharply angled incision just below the nodes. This will expose the maximum area of the stem's interior to the nourishing rooting medium.

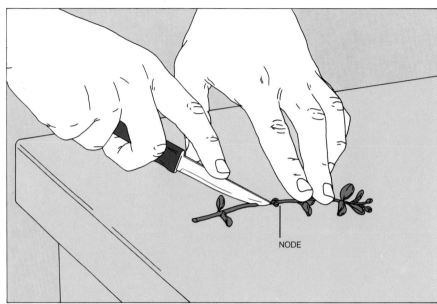

NODE

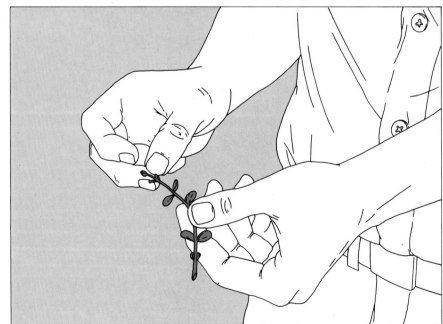

2 **Preparing the cutting for planting.** First, pinch off from the stem any flowers or seed heads; if allowed to remain, they would divert nutrients away from the roots that will form on the cutting. Also be certain that you trim away the leaves from any section of the stem that will be placed under the ground; buried foliage is liable to rot, providing a breeding ground for bacteria. Just before planting the cutting, dip its end into water, and then into plant hormone powder, making sure that only the base comes into contact with the powder.

3 **Planting the cuttings.** Fill a tray to about 25 mm from the top with moistened rooting medium. Then, using a small sharp stick or a pencil, poke holes in the medium just deep enough to cover two or three nodes on the stems of the cuttings. Set each of the cuttings in a hole, tamp the rooting medium down around it, and water the entire tray thoroughly but gently. Cover the tray with a sheet of glass or clear plastic.

Keep the tray in a warm room and out of direct sunlight until the roots are firmly established, then remove the glass to avoid "damping off". As a rule, the appearance of new leaves is a good indication that the cuttings are ready to be moved outdoors. Plant them in a prepared bed, exactly as you would set in new plants *(page 55)*.

Propagation by Division

1 **Uprooting the plants.** Using a hand fork, dig out a clump of plants from a dense growth of ground covers. As you raise the clump, guide the roots away from the tines of the fork with your free hand. The clump should contain enough stems to produce about 10 new plants.

2 **Separating the plants.** Rinse away soil from the clump so that you expose the roots; carefully pull the clump apart. Discard wilted or yellowish-looking plants, return two or three of the plants to their original hole, and set the rest in a new hole and water them thoroughly.

Coping with Slopes

A slope lends character and individuality to a home and its surroundings. A gentle grade, for example, can lead a visitor's eye to the front door; a contoured mound in the back garden can create a pleasant vista; a sharp embankment can separate the house from the street. But slopes can at the same time present some of the most challenging problems in landscaping.

Unplanted slopes which are exposed to heavy rain will almost certainly fall victim to soil erosion. Although grasses often grow well on slopes, manoeuvring a lawn mower over hilly terrain is awkward and hazardous. Swift-growing ground covers, with deep roots to hold the soil and thick leaves to catch and disperse water, are often the ideal solution.

The first rule of growing ground covers on any slope is to position the plants in staggered rows, thus creating a diamond-shaped pattern that will prevent water from washing straight down the slope in furrows. Mulch the entire area before setting in new plants: this protects the soil and helps keep weeds at bay.

On moderate slopes of 20 degrees or less, plant ground covers in shallow trenches dug across the bed, which will help to retain mulch and catch water. On slopes steeper than 20 degrees, use only the fastest-growing types of ground cover, such as periwinkle, and plant them very close together. Add an extra layer of mulch or a covering of netting to the ground before planting to help hold the soil until the roots are firmly established.

Very steep slopes may require terracing or even a retaining wall *(pages 28–31)*, and you can enhance the natural charm of a stone retaining wall by creating a rock garden in its crevices. A number of small, rambling plants, for instance catmint, thrive in an environment of rooting medium packed in the cracks between the masonry.

Planting in trenches. Beginning at the top of the slope, dig shallow trenches across the bed. If the trench goes down as far as the subsoil, dig in a structure-improving soil conditioner, such as compost *(pages 34–35)*. Mulch each trench and position the plants or seedlings in staggered rows.

Finishing touches for a retaining wall. To prepare a stone wall as a host for plants, first loosely fill the raked-out cracks between the stones with garden soil. Using a long-handled wooden spoon, tamp the soil 25 to 50 mm into the crevices in the front of the wall and then stuff chunks of a rooting medium such as moss peat into the spaces. After poking holes in the rooting medium with your finger or with a small pointed stick, set the plants into the holes and tamp the rooting medium around them gently. Water the plants with a fine mist from a hand-held hose.

A Selection of Ground Covers

	Special uses				Soil		Light		Special traits				Height			Foliage colour		Propagation methods		
	Frost-sensitive	Frost-tolerant	Slopes	Rock gardens	Moist	Dry	Partial shade	Full sun	Flowers or fruit	Climber	Rapid growth	Easy maintenance	Under 200 mm	200 to 400 mm	Over 400 mm	Green	Grey-green	Cuttings	Division	Layering
Evergreen																				
ACHILLEA TOMENTOSA (woolly yarrow)		●		●		●	●	●			●	●		●		●		●	●	
ARCTOSTAPHYLOS UVA-URSI (bearberry)		●	●			●		●				●		●		●		●	●	●
ARENARIA BALEARICA (Corsican sandwort)	●			●	●		●		●		●		●			●			●	
ARMERIA MARITIMA (common thrift)		●		●				●	●					●		●			●	
CALLUNA VULGARIS (Scotch heather)		●	●		●			●				●		●	●	●		●	●	
CEANOTHUS GRISEUS HORIZONTALIS (Carmel creeper)	●		●				●	●	●					●	●	●		●		
CERASTIUM TOMENTOSUM (snow-in-summer)		●		●		●	●	●	●		●	●	●				●	●	●	
ERICA CARNEA (winter heath)		●	●		●			●				●		●		●			●	●
FICUS PUMILA (evergreen fig)	●		●					●		●	●	●		●		●		●		●
FRAGARIA INDICA (alpine strawberry)		●			●		●		●		●	●		●		●		●		
GAULTHERIA PROCUMBENS (creeping wintergreen checkerberry)		●			●	●	●		●		●	●		●		●			●	●
HEDERA HELIX 'HIBERNICA' (Irish ivy)		●	●	●	●				●	●	●	●	●			●		●		
IBERIS SEMPERVIRENS (evergreen candytuft)		●					●	●	●			●		●		●		●	●	
JUNIPERUS HORIZONTALIS (creeping juniper)		●	●			●					●	●				●	●	●		
LIRIOPE MUSCARI (lily-turf)		●					●				●		●	●		●			●	
MAHONIA REPENS (creeping mahonia)		●	●		●			●	●		●	●		●		●		●	●	
PACHYSANDRA TERMINALIS (Japanese pachysandra)		●	●		●			●			●	●		●		●		●	●	
SAXIFRAGA STOLONIFERA (mother of thousands)	●			●		●		●			●	●	●			●			●	●
TAXUS BACCATA 'REPANDENS' (spreading English yew)		●		●								●		●	●	●		●		●
THYMUS SERPYLLUM (wild thyme)		●				●	●	●	●		●	●	●			●			●	
VINCA MINOR (lesser periwinkle)		●	●		●		●		●		●	●	●			●		●	●	
Deciduous																				
ARTEMISIA SCHMIDTIANA (silver mound artemisia)		●				●	●	●			●		●			●	●	●	●	
BERBERIS THUNBERGII (Japanese barberry)		●	●				●		●	●	●	●		●	●	●				
CONVALLARIA MAJALIS (lily of the valley)		●		●	●		●		●			●		●		●			●	
CORNUS CANADENSIS (creeping dogwood)		●		●	●		●				●	●	●			●			●	
CORONILLA VARIA (crown vetch)		●	●					●			●	●		●	●	●			●	
COTONEASTER ADPRESSUS (cotoneaster)		●	●				●					●		●		●		●		●
EPIMEDIUM GRANDIFLORUM (epimedium)		●		●		●	●		●			●		●		●			●	
GALIUM ODORATUM (sweet woodruff)		●		●		●	●				●	●		●		●			●	
NEPETA MUSSINII (mauve catmint)		●				●	●	●			●	●		●		●	●	●		
ROSA 'MAX GRAF' (Max Graf rose)		●				●	●				●			●	●	●		●		●
Semi-evergreen																				
AJUGA REPTANS (bugle)		●		●			●		●		●	●	●			●		●		
ANTHEMIS NOBILIS (chamomile)		●						●			●	●		●		●		●		
FESTUCA OVINA 'GLAUCA' (blue fescue)		●			●		●				●		●			●		●		
HELIANTHEMUM NUMMULARIUM (rock rose)		●		●			●	●			●		●			●		●	●	
HELXINE SOLEIROLII (baby's tears)	●			●		●					●	●	●			●		●	●	
HYPERICUM CALYCINUM (St. John's-wort)		●	●					●			●	●		●		●		●	●	
MENTHA REQUIENII (Corsican mint)		●		●	●			●	●		●		●			●			●	
OPHIOPOGON JAPONICUS (lily grass)	●			●				●			●	●	●			●		●		
PHLOX SUBULATA (moss phlox)		●		●			●	●	●		●	●	●			●		●	●	
ROSA WICHURAIANA (memorial rose)		●	●			●	●	●	●	●	●			●		●		●		●

Choosing a ground cover. This chart lists 41 common ground covers by their Latin and English names, grouped according to foliage type—evergreen, deciduous or semi-evergreen. The first two columns in the chart indicate whether or not the plant is tolerant of frost. Non-tolerant plants should only be planted in areas which are free of ground frost in winter.

Light and soil requirements are indicated by dots in the appropriate columns; these columns are left blank for plants that thrive in both moist and dry soil or in sunny and shaded positions. Many species have more than one special trait or can be propagated by more than one method; for these, multiple dots are entered.

Fast-Growing Climbers for a Dramatic Display

Because they can be remarkably fast growing and hardy, climbers can cover large areas quickly. What is more, they create a uniquely dramatic green or variegated display because of the manner of their growth. Sending sinuous stems upwards and outwards, climbers mature as long ribbons of foliage that can be trained and pruned to grow either on solid walls or on open fences *(opposite and page 62)*, or on such special supports as trellises, pergolas and archways *(pages 116–121)*.

Depending on how they are supported and where they are positioned, climbers can accentuate attractive landscaping features, screen unattractive ones, provide leafy shade over a sitting area, or offer a lush backdrop for decorative shrubs and flowers. With no support at all, certain climbers can serve as ground covers for areas of the garden too steep or too shady for a conventional lawn. In general, climbers are ideal plants for compact areas because they take up very little ground space for their abundance of foliage. They are also ideal for new gardens, where they fill an area long before slower-growing shrubs and trees can take over.

Many garden climbers are descended from tropical plants and grow outdoors only in warm climates; others, including such favourites as ivy and winter creeper, are hardy in cool climates. The chart on page 63 lists the climbers that are most widely available, along with indications of each plant's most important features: is the foliage variegated or uniformly green? Is the climber annual or perennial? Evergreen or deciduous? Frost-tolerant or frost-sensitive? In some cases, the chart lists characteristics that appear to be contradictory. Some climbing plants that are perennials in warm climates become annuals in cool climates and must be replanted every year. Similarly, some evergreen climbers are deciduous in cooler areas.

The methods by which these plants climb are an important consideration in choosing a specific climbing plant to fill a landscaping need. Botanists distinguish among more than 30 different techniques that climbers have developed to compensate for their inability to support themselves. Landscape designers and gardeners generally combine the 30 into the three major groupings listed in the chart.

Twiners, including akebia and wisteria, grow upwards in a spiral, wrapping their stems round upright posts and vertical trellis supports. Clingers, such as Boston ivy and grape ivy, send out sticky rootlets or finger-like tendrils to hold fast to vertical and horizontal surfaces alike. And leaners, such as roses and most jasmines, do not actually climb, but arch upwards and droop unless they are draped over an upright support or secured with twine or with plant ties.

Almost all climbers begin to grow soon after their deep root systems have had time to develop. The waiting period is brief for annuals—morning glories are a very fast-starting species of climber—but some of the perennials, such as wisteria, may need two or three years to get ready. If you want immediate shade from a new pergola, consider planting annuals adjacent to perennials for the first year or two.

Rates of growth vary considerably. In a single season of growth, the aptly named winter creeper extends itself only a few centimetres; the silver fleece vine can reach out as far as 9 metres. For purposes of comparison, the chart defines slow growers as climbers that grow less than 300 mm a year; medium growers from 300 to 1500 mm and fast growers more than 1500 mm. Of course, differences in care, watering and climate can affect growth rates considerably; use the chart to get a relative idea of what to expect from a given species of climbing plant.

Most climbers grow best in moist but well-drained soil that is mildly acid, between 6.5 and 7 pH. Annuals are usually planted as seeds and can often be started indoors during the winter, then transplanted outdoors in the spring. Perennials are usually sold as potted plants one or two years old and should be placed in a 600 to 900 mm-deep mixture of soil and low-nitrogen fertilizer (5-10-5) according to the manufacturer's instructions. These formulations initially stimulate root and stem development at the expense of foliage growth, but the trade-off is worthwhile for the future health of the plants.

Water newly planted climbers well, and provide them with a thorough soaking every seven to ten days during the growing season unless there has been a heavy fall of rain. During the hottest months, add a layer of mulch round the base of the plants to retain moisture.

Left alone, most climbers tend to extend stems straight up without branching; they must be tied to horizontal supports and carefully pruned to promote horizontal growth. When plants are young, pinch off the stem tips just above the growth buds to encourage branching and dense growth. On mature plants, cut away excess growth at least once a year—preferably in late winter or early spring when the plant is dormant—and remove some of the stems near the centre of the plant to stimulate growth in the outer stems.

Climbers are notably healthy plants, requiring little protection from insects and disease. For most, an occasional spraying with a brisk jet of water is sufficient to discourage insects. It may be necessary to use insecticides to repel severe attacks of aphids and to control scale insects, which damage the leaves and stems.

Ties That Bind

Supporting climbing plants. To attach a climber to a support, use soft, flexible ties and, starting at the base of the plant, bind each stem loosely to avoid disrupting the flow of sap. The figure-of-eight loop *(top, left)* keeps the stem from chafing against the support. Fasten the tie first to the support, then to the stem. Alternatively, place a U-shaped length of plastic-coated wire lightly round the stem, on the side opposite to the support *(top, right)*. Then bend the ends and wrap them several times round the support. Check the ties frequently; loosen them as the stems thicken.

To train a lightweight climber to grow in a certain pattern against a wall, especially if you want it to frame the corner of a window or door, drape the stem over a hook set in an adhesive disc *(centre, left)*. This method is particularly useful for a climber such as Cape honeysuckle which has no mechanism for attaching itself. For a plant with a woody stem, use a special wall-mount nail fitted with a strip of soft, non-corrosive metal such as lead. Drive the nail into the wall or fence (it will work on both wood and masonry), and bend the strip round the stem of the climber *(centre, right)*.

A light climber such as a clematis can be laced to a fence. Starting at the bottom, feed a roll of soft twine or plastic-coated wire through screw hooks set in the fence at regular intervals *(bottom, left)*. Leave extra twine at the top so that, as it grows, more levels of support can be added. If the plant dies back in winter, unlace the twine and lace the new growth the following year. For a heavier climber on a masonry wall, use horizontal rows of plastic-coated galvanized wire *(bottom, right)*. String the wire between vine eyes set no more than 1.8 metres apart and secured with expanding masonry anchor bolts.

Creating a Wall Covering of Ivy

Establishing the plant. To create an ivy-covered wall that is attractive, healthy and easy to maintain, plant a rooted cutting of common or English ivy 150 to 250 mm long at the base of the wall in spring. Use a soil enriched with humus to improve water retention, and water well in the weeks following planting. Encourage the ivy to grow upright against the wall; do not prune. The following spring, cut all the shoots back to the ground *(shown in grey, far left)*.

In late spring, after the ivy has sent up strong new shoots, select four of the most vigorous *(left)* and train them upright against the wall in the shape of a fan, guiding them if necessary *(page 61)*. Prune away all other growth.

Training the shoots. The following spring, cut back the trained shoots by one-third of their length to stimulate lateral branching. Remove any new vertical shoots that appear between the four main shoots *(far left)*.

Later in the year, lateral branches will begin to fill in bare areas between the trained shoots *(left)*. Each spring, cut back the new top growth by one-third. Remove new vertical shoots at ground level and cut off stems that project out from the wall. In this way, one ivy cutting can cover 2 square metres of wall with a single layer of neat foliage.

Characteristics of Climbers

Plant	Frost-sensitive	Frost-tolerant	Ground cover	Shade	Screen	Full sun	Partial shade	Deciduous	Evergreen	Annual	Perennial	Fruits/berries	Flowers	Fast	Medium	Slow	Clinger	Leaner	Twiner	Green	Variegated
			Uses			**Light**		**Traits**						**Growth rate**			**Climbing means**			**Foliage colour**	
AKEBIA QUINATA (**five-leaf akebia**)		●	●	●	●	●	●	●			●	●	●		●				●	●	
AMPELOPSIS BREVIPEDUNCULATA (**porcelain ampelopsis**)		●	●	●	●		●			●	●	●		●			●			●	
BIGNONIA CAPREOLATA (**cross-vine**)	●		●		●	●		●	●		●		●	●			●				●
BOUGAINVILLEA SPECTABILIS (**Brazilian bougainvillea**)	●			●	●		●		●		●		●	●				●		●	
CAMPSIS RADICANS (**trumpet creeper**)		●		●	●		●	●			●		●	●			●			●	
CISSUS RHOMBIFOLIA (**grape ivy**)	●			●	●		●		●		●			●					●	●	
CLEMATIS FLORIDA 'DUCHESS OF EDINBURGH' (**clematis 'Duchess of Edinburgh'**)		●		●	●	●	●		●		●		●	●			●			●	
CLEMATIS X JACKMANII (**clematis Jackmanii**)		●		●	●	●	●		●		●		●	●			●			●	
CLEMATIS MONTANA (**clematis montana**)		●		●	●	●	●		●		●		●	●			●			●	
CLEMATIS X 'NELLY MOSER' (**clematis 'Nelly Moser'**)		●		●	●	●	●		●		●		●	●			●			●	
CLERODENDRUM THOMSONIAE (**bleeding heart**)	●			●		●		●			●		●		●				●	●	
COBAEA SCANDENS (**cup-and-saucer vine**)		●		●	●	●		●	●	●	●		●	●			●			●	
EUONYMUS FORTUNEI (**common winter creeper**)		●	●		●		●		●	●	●				●	●	●			●	
FICUS PUMILA (**creeping fig**)	●			●	●		●		●		●				●		●			●	
GELSEMIUM SEMPERVIRENS (**false jasmine**)	●		●	●	●		●		●		●		●	●				●		●	
HEDERA CANARIENSIS 'VARIEGATA' (**Algerian variegated ivy**)	●			●	●		●		●		●			●			●				●
HEDERA HELIX (**common or English ivy**)		●	●	●		●			●		●				●		●			●	
HIBBERTIA SCANDENS (**Guinea gold vine**)	●			●	●			●			●		●	●					●	●	
HYDRANGEA PETIOLARIS (**climbing hydrangea**)		●		●	●	●					●		●	●			●			●	
IPOMOEA TRICOLOR (**morning glory**)		●	●		●	●		●		●	●		●	●				●	●	●	
JASMINUM OFFICINALE (**white jasmine**)	●			●		●	●	●			●		●	●					●	●	
LANTANA MONTEVIDENSIS (**trailing lantana**)	●		●			●		●	●	●	●		●	●					●	●	
LONICERA X HECKROTTII (**goldflame honeysuckle**)		●	●			●	●	●			●		●	●					●	●	
LONICERA JAPONICA 'HALLIANA' (**Halliana honeysuckle**)		●	●		●		●		●		●		●	●					●	●	
LONICERA SEMPERVIRENS (**trumpet honeysuckle**)	●			●		●	●	●			●	●	●	●					●	●	
PARTHENOCISSUS QUINQUEFOLIA (**Virginia creeper**)		●	●		●		●	●			●	●		●			●				●
PARTHENOCISSUS TRICUSPIDATA (**Boston ivy**)		●	●		●		●	●			●	●		●			●			●	
PASSIFLORA CAERULEA (**passion flower**)	●			●	●	●		●	●		●		●	●					●	●	
PLUMBAGO CAPENSIS (**Cape plumbago**)	●			●	●	●			●		●		●	●				●		●	
POLYGONUM AUBERTII (**silver fleece vine**)		●		●	●	●		●			●		●	●					●	●	
ROSA BANKSIAE (**Banksian rose**)		●		●	●	●	●		●		●		●	●				●		●	
ROSA 'BLAZE' (**blaze rose**)		●		●	●	●			●		●		●	●				●		●	
ROSA WICHURAIANA (**memorial rose**)		●	●		●	●	●	●			●		●		●			●		●	
SOLANDRA GUTTATA (**Goldcup chalice vine**)	●			●	●			●			●		●	●				●		●	
TECOMARIA CAPENSIS (**Cape honeysuckle**)	●			●	●	●			●		●		●	●				●		●	
THUNBERGIA ALATA (**black-eyed-Susan vine**)	●		●			●		●	●	●	●		●	●				●		●	
TRACHELOSPERMUM JASMINOIDES (**star jasmine**)	●		●	●	●		●		●		●		●		●				●	●	
VITIS LABRUSCA (**fox grape**)		●		●	●	●		●			●	●		●			●				●
WISTERIA SINENSIS (**Chinese wisteria**)		●			●	●		●			●	●	●	●					●	●	

Choosing a climbing plant. This chart lists, in alphabetical order, 39 selected species of climbing plant by their Latin names, followed by their common English names. Read the dots horizontally to determine the characteristics of a particular plant; read the lines vertically to assemble a choice of plants with certain characteristics in common. Note that in two of the categories, Uses and Traits, the characteristics of a single species of climbing plant may be indicated by more than one dot; in the remaining categories, one dot signifies the predominant characteristic of that plant. For additional information on how climbing plants can be used as ground covers, refer to the chart on page 59.

3 Tall Trees and Massed Shrubs

A neat cut that heals cleanly. The stubby, curved cutting blade of a pair of lopping shears slices easily through an unwanted branch; the same bevelled blade will also trim the dead stub to the left below it, leaving a clean wound that resists infection and heals easily. Such judicious pruning shapes trees and shrubs, fosters thick foliage and, above all, protects the plants' health.

Small garden plants tend to be prized for either their beauty or their utility. Trees and their smaller cousins, the shrubs, combine both virtues—and more. They create a variety of delights: the rustle of wind in branches; the fragrance of blossoms and foliage; and a rich range of colour, from the pale green buds of spring to the lush growth of summer and the finale of fiery autumn. But they have practical uses too. Trees can screen a biting winter wind, shade a patio or lawn from summer sun, yield a harvest of nuts or fruit; shrubs serve as borders, windbreaks or high privacy hedges.

Trees in particular have another, more elusive virtue. Their qualities and long lives inspire a deep human bond. People plant saplings for posterity, cherish mature trees for generations and mourn the passing of a gnarled, weatherbeaten hardwood almost as a death in the family. There are practical as well as sentimental reasons for this solicitude. Unlike smaller plants, which may require weekly care but seldom give major trouble, large woody specimens need something like the foresight and preventive care that physicians give their human patients. A sapling that develops a sharp V-shaped crotch rather than a U-shaped one should be pruned while young *(pages 66–69)*, for such a crotch will weaken the mature tree. Leaves may be scorched by a nearby barbecue grill, impairing their ability to convert sunlight into energy. Root beds, which extend well beyond the circle marked by the outermost branches of a tree or hedge, must be protected from several hazards. Slight changes in contour or drainage can inundate the roots or deprive them of water, a patio or footpath can effectively suffocate any roots below it, and heavy construction machinery compacts the soil so densely that nutrients and water cannot reach the roots. Damage from such insidious hazards is slow to develop, but cumulative and eventually deadly.

Caring for trees and shrubs requires not only preventive care but vigilance and quick intervention. A broken or diseased branch must be cut off before infection can enter the ragged stump or invade healthy wood; if you suspect fungus or disease, clean the pruning tools afterwards with disinfectant. Cuts and bruises of any sort—from nails, ropes, lawn mowers and so on—expose the wood to pests and disease; trim away the ragged bark with a knife, leaving a vertical oval with a neat edge between the healthy bark and the wound. Before lopping or pruning large branches, or if you have no alternative other than to remove a tree completely, consult your local authority first. In some areas, you will need permission before carrying out major tree surgery of this kind. Potential attacks by pests and disease can be forestalled by chemical sprays *(page 70)*. These measures entail only a modest investment of time, but they ensure a rich return both in pleasure and usefulness—which in some cases lasts literally for generations—from the dominant landmarks of a garden.

Techniques for Keeping a Tree in Good Health

Trees are rightly prized for their stature, their beauty of leaf, their fragrant flowering in springtime and their cascades of red and gold in autumn—but they offer more than aesthetic value alone. Deciduous trees on the side of a house facing the sun shield it on hot summer days. Evergreens form a barrier to the harsh winds of winter. And a row of low-growing trees along a busy road screens out traffic.

Like the houses they protect and adorn, trees need regular—sometimes professional—care. Filling a hollow cavity or bracing limbs with guy wires requires expertise; therefore, only a specialist should attempt such jobs. Similarly, cutting limbs while perched high in a tree is dangerous for a novice; sawn limbs often kick back in an unpredictable way and can knock an unwary worker to the ground.

Fortunately, the routine maintenance chores of pruning, fertilizing and pest control fall within the home owner's abilities. These three essentials of tree husbandry are especially crucial for young plants; a well-maintained sapling will grow into a strong, well-formed tree that will seldom need professional care.

Pruning improves the health of a tree but, like all surgery, it must be done judiciously. No matter how carefully a pruning cut is made it wounds the tree; the key to good pruning lies in making precise and minimal cuts that help the tree to use its natural healing mechanisms.

To defend itself, a tree surrounds a wound with specialized cells and produces chemical barriers that prevent disease-causing organisms from invading healthy tissue. These cells and chemicals develop at the base of each branch in a swollen area called the branch collar. Pruning a branch flush to the trunk, as recommended in the past, destroys protective cells in the collar and the wound closes slowly, if at all. Cutting too far from the trunk leaves a stub that can conduct disease-bearing microorganisms into the tree; impeded by the stub, the tissue of protective cells will not be able to close the wound. Only cuts made just outside the collar at the correct angle *(opposite page, below)* will close properly.

Painting a pruning wound, a technique formerly believed to aid the closing process, offers no benefit to the tree, and heavy coatings retard closure. However, a thin coat of zinc-based tree paint has a certain cosmetic value and it will do no harm.

For the varied sizes and locations of tree limbs, you will need special pruning tools. Those illustrated on pages 68–69—a pruning knife, lopping shears, pruning saw and tree pruner—will handle all the pruning chores you are likely to attempt. Keep the blade of any pruning tool razor-sharp *(page 12)*, so that it slices limbs cleanly without tearing or compressing the wood. To protect yourself from the blade, wear heavy gloves when handling the tools. Wear eye protection when cutting overhead.

In general, the best pruning seasons are late winter and early spring, before the buds open. Flowering trees, however, should be pruned just after the flowers fade, and broken or diseased branches should be removed immediately they are spotted.

To maintain vigorous normal growth, trees need a variety of chemical elements from the soil. The best way to supply a garden tree with essential elements is to fertilize it. Fertilizer can be poured dry into holes close to the roots, or sprayed in liquid form directly on to the leaves. Good dry fertilizers include manufactured mixes and organic materials, such as hoof and bone meal or dried blood, which are mixed with soil, sand or moss peat and dug into holes around the tree. They should be applied every year or two in early spring.

Spraying proprietary liquid fertilizer directly on to the leaves brings quick results. This method, which is known as foliar fertilization will perk up a tree in a week, but its dramatic effects are short-lived. It is best to use a combination of foliar and root fertilization.

Trees which have been regularly pruned and fertilized are fairly resistant to most insects and diseases, but even a healthy tree can succumb. If a tree looks sickly or harbours pests you do not recognize, seek advice from your local authority or from a professional tree surgeon. The prescription is likely to be a spray-on chemical.

Chemical sprays are strong medicines that must be handled with care, but you can spray a tree up to 8 metres tall safely with the equipment shown on page 70. For a larger tree, call in a professional.

For trees up to 3 metres tall, use a pressurized canister—a 5 or 10 litre plastic or steel container with a built-in pressure pump. For taller trees, use a garden-hose attachment that automatically mixes insecticide and water; the sprayer itself is small, but it can deliver up to 25 litres of solution between fillings.

Before using any insecticide or other spray, check the by-laws governing chemical spraying in your area. Study the instructions and cautions on the label. Most insecticides must be mixed with water; dilute them exactly as directed. While spraying a tree, wear long sleeves, gloves, goggles and a hat. Keep children and pets out of the area, and do not permit them to walk near recently sprayed trees. And avoid spraying in windy weather.

If you want to try a treatment that is non-toxic to pets and humans, a spray of tar oil—a mixture of mineral oil and water—is an alternative to strong chemical insecticides for the control of certain pests. Sprayed on a tree in early spring, before leaves emerge, the mixture coats and smothers aphids, scales, mites and insect eggs. Read the label directions carefully: the oil can damage evergreens and certain species of beech, birch and maple.

Biological controls consisting of a pest's natural enemies offer another alternative to chemicals. A single ladybird will eat four dozen aphids a day; an invisible bacterium attacks gypsy-moth caterpillars but is harmless to other organisms. Ask your local garden centre for advice on obtaining such pest fighters in your area.

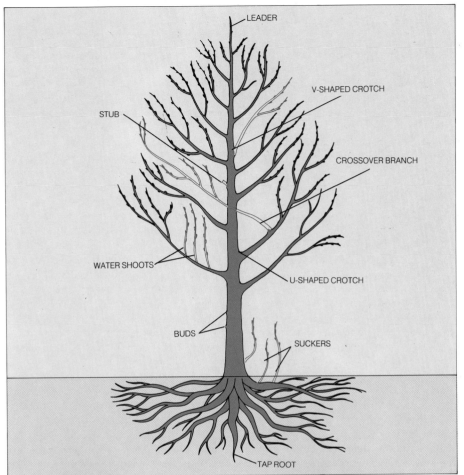

LEADER

V-SHAPED CROTCH

STUB

CROSSOVER BRANCH

WATER SHOOTS

U-SHAPED CROTCH

BUDS

SUCKERS

TAP ROOT

How to Prune a Tree

The basic guidelines. On a well-formed young tree, a straight central branch called the leader extends above all the other branches; the main limbs have U-shaped crotches, are evenly distributed round the trunk and are spaced at least 300 mm apart. In order to maintain this strong, balanced framework, you must prune away the undesirable features, represented in white.

Remove any branches with a tight, V-shaped crotch; such a joint is inherently weak. Slender shoots called suckers or water shoots, which grow from the limbs, trunk or roots of the tree and put out no lateral branches, are not part of the natural branch pattern; cut off these shoots and any buds on the trunk. Remove branch stubs and dead or broken limbs, and thin out small branches that grow in towards the trunk or across larger limbs; these crossover branches will eventually rub against their neighbours, wearing away bark and causing wounds.

Mature trees have a few additional pruning requirements. Thin out inner branches periodically to admit light. On a deciduous tree, remove low limbs that prevent you from walking under the tree. The lower limbs on evergreen trees are usually left in place. On any tree, remove all dead, diseased or broken branches.

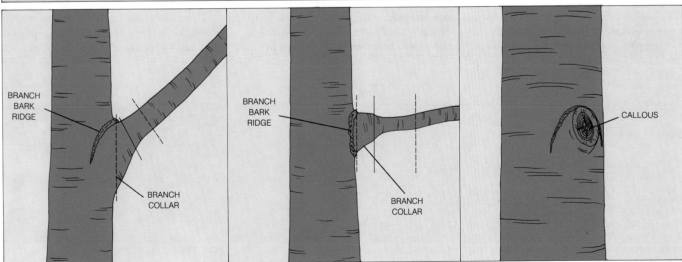

BRANCH BARK RIDGE

BRANCH COLLAR

BRANCH BARK RIDGE

BRANCH COLLAR

CALLOUS

Proper pruning cuts. The structure of a tree dictates the correct spot and angle for cutting off a branch. A growing branch develops a thickened collar at its base, and a dark, raised saddle called the branch bark ridge forms on the parent branch or trunk. To remove a branch, cut outside of and at an opposing angle to the ridge, as indicated by the solid line *(above, left)*; do not cut into the collar itself or into the ridge, and do not cut so far along that it will leave a stub *(dotted line)*.

On evergreens and very young deciduous trees, the bark ridge may encircle the base of the branch, and the collar may be especially large and pronounced *(above, middle)*. In such a case, make a straight cut just outside the collar and parallel to the bark ridge *(solid line)*; be sure not to leave a stub beyond the collar, and take care not to cut into the ridge or the collar *(dotted lines)*. In a year or so, the edge of a pruning wound should form a hard callous *(above, right)*, and eventually this hard growth will close over the cut. If the callous does not form or forms incompletely, the cut may have been incorrect or the tree may be too old or weak to respond well.

Two Tools for Small-Scale Pruning

A knife to flick off shoots. Use a pruning knife to slice off buds and small branches up to 6 mm thick. Wearing heavy gardening gloves, set the knife's curved cutting edge on the top of a shoot; press your thumb against the bottom of the shoot, and turn the knife handle downwards with a twist of your wrist *(arrow).*

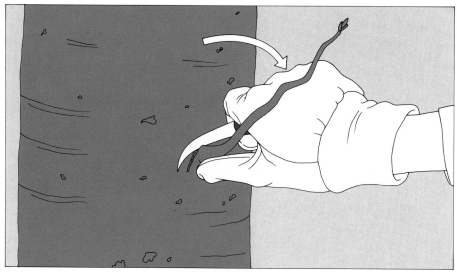

Cutting off small branches. To cut off a branch up to 25 mm thick, set the cutting blade of a pair of lopping shears on top of the limb, with the side of the blade against the trunk or supporting branch; then angle the lower blade away from the branch bark ridge and the branch collar, and bring the handles of the shears together in a single smooth motion. Do not twist the shears or use them to pull the branch away from the tree, and do not make repeated hacking cuts; if you find that you are resorting to any of these manoeuvres, either the branch is too large for the tool or the blade is too blunt for the job.

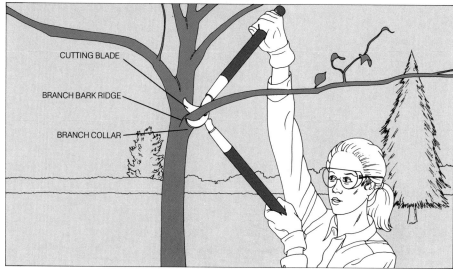

Sawing Off a Large Branch

1 **Removing the branch.** Before cutting a·branch up to 75 mm thick, trim away secondary limbs to lighten the branch and to keep it from catching in the tree as it falls, then use a pruning saw to cut the branch itself in two separate stages. First, saw half way through the underside of the branch, about 30 cm from the trunk; this cut will keep the bark from tearing when the branch falls. Next, about 25 mm out from the first cut, saw down through the branch from the top; when the second cut is half way through the branch the limb will snap off, leaving a stub.

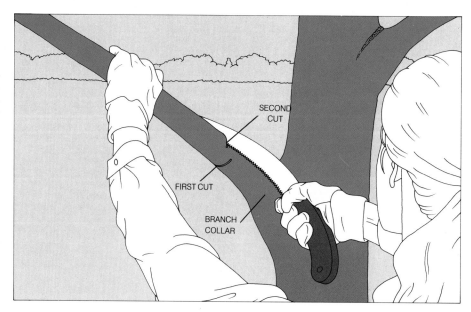

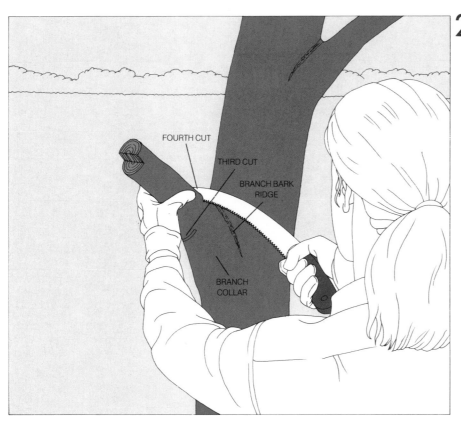

2 Trimming the stub. Saw a 25 mm cut through the underside of the stub, just outside the branch collar and at an angle opposite to that of the branch bark ridge. Supporting the stub with one hand, set the saw blade on the crotch of the stub *(left)*, just outside the branch bark ridge; saw downwards at an angle to meet the upward cut.

FOURTH CUT

THIRD CUT

BRANCH BARK RIDGE

BRANCH COLLAR

SAW BLADE

HOOK

CUTTING BLADE

PULLEYS

POLE

Pole Tools for High Pruning

Extendable shears. To reach branches up to 5 metres overhead, tree pruners have a telescoping metal or plastic shaft; the cord that works the cutting blade has a double pulley to increase leverage. Place the hook, located above the blade, over the base of the branch; wrap the cord once round the pole to keep the shaft from bending, and pull on the cord to move the blade. It may be difficult to position the blade exactly for a properly angled cut, but be sure to cut close enough to the branch collar so that you do not leave a stub. If the cut branch hangs in the tree, pull it down with the head of the pruners, but try not to break other branches. Tree pruners will cut through branches which are 10 to 25 mm thick, depending on the hardness of the wood.

Cut high branches up to 100 mm thick with the saw attachment *(inset)* of a pair of tree pruners. Set the saw's teeth against the side of the branch and move the blade in short up-and-down strokes; if the saw binds, start again from the other side. As with the tree pruners, it is hard to position the blade properly in relation to the branch collar and bark ridge, but you should be able to execute a smooth, straight cut without leaving a stub. If the branch is thicker than 25 mm, wear a hard hat.

Fertilizing Trees
Through Leaf and Root

Using a garden-hose sprayer. Pour the amount of liquid fertilizer recommended by the manufacturer into the sprayer reservoir. Add water until the mixture reaches the level on the litres scale that indicates the amount of spray solution needed. Screw on the spray mechanism, close the water valve and gently shake the sprayer.

Connect the sprayer to a garden hose and open the tap. With the sprayer pointed at the tree, open the water valve on the sprayer. To control the length of the spray, adjust the garden-hose tap. When spraying tar oil, adjust the sprayer nozzle for a narrow stream, and saturate the trunk and limbs.

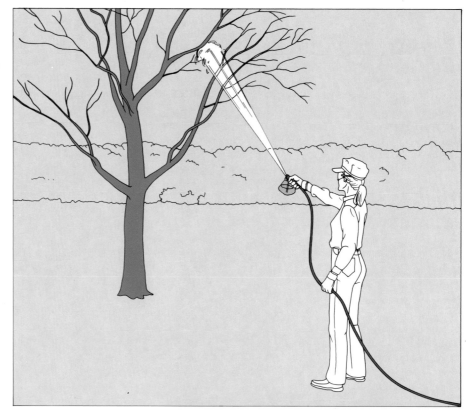

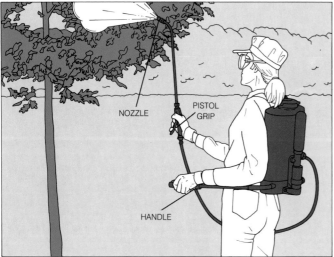

Using a pressurized knapsack sprayer. To fill the sprayer, pour in some water and add liquid fertilizer or insecticide. Pour in the rest of the water needed to dilute the chemical. If you are using a powder, combine it with water in a bucket before pouring it into the sprayer to make sure it is completely mixed. Screw on the lid, and vigorously raise and lower the pump handle several times to pressurize the tank. As you spray, pump the handle each time the spray weakens. Aim the nozzle upwards and squeeze the pistol grip to saturate the undersides of leaves. Adjust the fineness of the spray, if necessary, by twisting the nozzle tip or changing nozzles, depending on the model.

Applying dry fertilizer. Lay a string or garden hose round the tree at the drip line—the line directly below the tree's outermost leaves. Mark a second circle about two-thirds of the way in from the drip line to the trunk, and a third circle about the same distance outside the drip line. Allowing about 10 holes for each 25 mm of the trunk's diameter, plan hole locations distributed evenly between the inner and outer circles *(inset)*.

Using a trowel, roll back a piece of turf, and make a hole 300 to 450 mm deep. Pour a cup of dry fertilizer mixed with an equal amount of soil, coarse sand or moss peat into each hole using a large funnel. Fold the grass back into place and tamp it down with your foot.

Safe Procedures for Removing Trees and Stumps

Despite all attempts to protect and care for them, trees sometimes have to be felled. Old age or decay can weaken a tree and make it unsafe, threatening damage to your house or a neighbouring property; or a tree may become so large and unwieldy that it eventually blocks light from a previously sunny room.

The most common cause of weakness in trees of any age is fungal decay. Trees should be inspected at regular intervals for signs of disease: dangerous decay in the roots is often indicated by fungal growths round the base of the tree, or by telltale thinning of foliage, dead wood at the top of the crown, or crumbling bark on the trunk. A tree with signs of decay does not always constitute a safety hazard, but if the decay has reached an advanced state, the tree will usually have to be felled.

Before starting work, check with your local authority about regulations relating to trees in your area. In a Conservation Area, you must inform your local authority of your intention to fell a tree six weeks before you plan to start.

Once you have approval to fell a tree, you must next make the work area safe.

Felling even a small tree is a potentially dangerous task, and requires careful planning. The felled tree will occupy a surprising amount of space, and branches can easily split away from the trunk as the tree hits the ground. If possible, you should mark out a danger zone with a radius of twice the height of the tree *(below)*; warn all bystanders to stay outside this area while felling is in progress. The felling of large trees should always be undertaken by a professional tree surgeon.

Next, decide the direction in which the tree is to fall—away from buildings and overhead wires, and from people and property. If the tree is standing in a confined space you may have to cut it down in sections, or to remove some of the branches before felling. Always wear a safety helmet, leather gloves and tough footwear while you work, and avoid felling in windy conditions—a strong gust of wind can easily cause a tree to fall before you are fully prepared, and in a direction other than intended. If you are in any doubt at all about safety—if, for example, the tree has a pronounced lean, an unbalanced crown, or contains a lot of dead or decayed ma-

terial—your best course is to consult a professional tree surgeon.

You must also decide before starting work how you wish to dispose of the stump. The quickest way to remove a stump from the ground is to use a winch *(page 73, above)*, but this may be difficult in a confined area where there is not enough room to anchor the free end of the winch. An alternative method is to hire a stump-chipping machine, which will reduce your stump to a pile of woodchips in a matter of minutes. If all you want to do is to prevent regrowth of the stump, cut it as close to the ground as possible, drill holes in it, then treat the exposed surface with chemicals to prevent further growth *(page 73, below)*.

Before you start work, make sure that any tools you are going to use are in good condition. A 450 mm bow saw is the safest and most versatile tool for felling smaller trees; a chain saw is dangerous and should not be used without professional help. An axe is also useful for chopping through the roots at the base of a tree when removing the stump, but is a difficult tool for the amateur to use effectively for cutting through a tree trunk.

Preparing to Fell

Keeping a safe distance. The clearance area for safe felling is a large circle whose radius is twice the height of the tree. The two areas of maximum safety—to be used as escape routes in case of immediate danger—are shown in the diagram on the right. To make sure that the tree falls in the required direction, attach a rope as high up the trunk as possible, using a non-slip knot. The rope should be at least twice as long as the tree is high, and a minimum of 8 mm in diameter. Get a helper to stand outside the felling area, in the direction of fall, ready to pull on the rope when the tree is ready to fall.

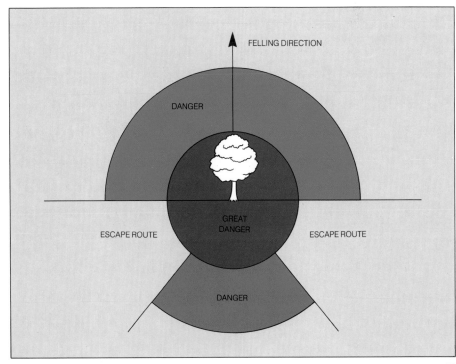

FELLING DIRECTION

DANGER

DANGER

GREAT
DANGER

ESCAPE ROUTE

ESCAPE ROUTE

The Safe Way to Fell a Tree

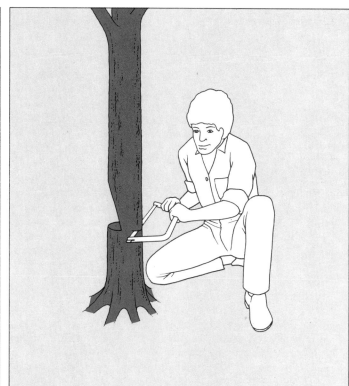

1 **Making the notch cut.** On the side of the tree facing the felling direction, remove a wedge-shaped section with a bow saw. Make the downward cut first at approximately 45 degrees into the tree trunk, then make a horizontal cut lower down the tree so that the two meet about a third of the way into the trunk.

2 **Making the felling cut.** With the bow saw make a horizontal cut on the opposite side of the trunk 25 mm above the base of the notch cut. Stop sawing about 25 mm from the back of the notch so the tree is supported by a "hinge" of wood.

3 **Bringing the tree down.** When you have completed sawing, move to the side of the tree, and signal to your assistant to pull steadily on the rope. Depending on the type of the wood and the thickness of your hinge, it may be necessary to make the felling cut deeper. Make sure that your assistant is informed and pulls only at your signal.

Dealing with Stumps

Using a winch. With a sharp spade dig a trench about 600 mm deep and one metre in radius round the stump. Uncover all the roots that radiate out and sever these with an axe or saw. At this point it may be possible to lever a small stump out without using a winch. If not, attach one cable or chain to the stump and another to a ground anchor or a nearby tree protected by thick pads of carpeting. Hook the movable cable of the winch to the cable round the stump, and attach the opposite end of the winch to the anchor cable or chain. Winch the stump over on its side, carefully cutting any roots as you do so.

Using chemicals. With a brace and bit, drill holes about 75 mm deep and 12 mm wide at approximately 50 mm intervals round the top of the stump. Using a funnel, pour in a strong solution of an oxidizing agent, such as sodium chlorate or ammonium sulphamate, taking care not to spill it on surrounding plants. Seal the holes with clay. The chemical should penetrate the stump, preventing it from producing new growth.

How to Move a Tree

A tree's size, weight and stability make it seem a permanent part of a landscape, but there are times when a tree must be moved. Small or young trees should be shifted out of the way of construction projects to protect their trunks and branches from injury, and prevent their roots from being compacted by heavy equipment; the trees can be stored safely and replanted when the work is finished. A mature tree might be relocated permanently to fit a new landscape plan, and some trees must be moved from locations dangerous to their health—areas with poor drainage, unfavourable soil or extreme wind.

Trees up to 3 metres tall with trunks up to 50 mm thick can be moved with relative ease and can be expected to prosper after the move. Larger trees, however, are unwieldy and are more vulnerable to shock; the job of moving them should be evaluated—and, generally, performed—by a professional tree surgeon.

The best time to move a deciduous tree is during its dormant period in late autumn or early spring, except when there is a ground frost; an evergreen should be moved in early spring or early autumn. If possible, cut the roots to their proper root-ball dimensions (*right, above*) up to a year in advance, so that new feeder roots have time to form before the tree is moved. Cut half the roots in one stage, and the other half six months later, but do not cut the tap root—the main support root that runs straight down into the ground—until it is time to move the tree. At this point the tree will no longer be able to support its full complement of branches and foliage; to make up for the lost root capacity, prune away about a third of the branches.

When the time comes to move the tree, cut the tap root and wrap the root ball in hessian, either tied with twine or pinned with 50 or 75 mm nails. Tying with twine is somewhat simpler for beginners. Use a biodegradable material, such as cotton or hemp, which disintegrates after the tree is replanted; do not use plastic or nylon string, which would eventually strangle the roots. Pinning the hessian calls for more skill, but it is easier in the long run, particularly on large trees, because it does not require tilting the heavy root ball.

Uprooting a Tree—Safely

1 **Pruning the roots.** Using a spade with a well-sharpened blade, sever the roots in a semi-circle 600 to 900 mm away from the trunk. Push the blade into the ground at an angle of approximately 30 degrees towards the trunk, so that the root ball will taper. Dig a trench about 450 mm deep, fill it with peat, and tread the surface down firmly. Six months later, follow the same procedure to complete the circle and fill with peat as before.

TAP ROOT

HESSIAN

2 **Digging out the tree.** Mark the north-facing side of the tree with a dab of paint to ensure that it will be correctly repositioned. Loosen the peat around the edge of the hole, then thrust the sharpened blade of a spade horizontally beneath the tree and sever the tap root and other large roots. Next, working with a helper, lift the tree by the root ball and place the root ball in the centre of a square of hessian.

Lifting an evergreen or any small tree with low branches may be easier if you work the hessian into the hole first, as for shrubs (*page 92*).

3 **Bagging the root ball.** To tie hessian round a root ball *(below, left)*, draw the fabric up round the ball on all sides, tucking in the excess; then secure the hessian round the trunk with several turns of a length of twine. Run the twine under the ball in several directions, tilting the tree to get the string beneath it. When you have bound the root ball into a neat package, turn the twine round the trunk several more times and tie it.

To pin hessian round a root ball *(below, right)*, gather a corner of the fabric, folding the excess under, and pull it up tightly over the ball. Push a 50 or 75 mm nail carefully through the fabric parallel to the top of the root ball, then turn the nail back and thrust it through the fabric and into the ball. Continue gathering and pinning sections of hessian in this way until you have bound the root ball snugly on all sides.

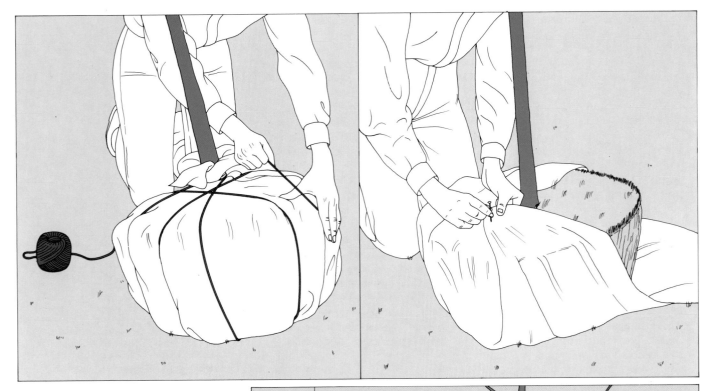

4 **Storing the tree.** At a spot that is shady and protected from wind, dig a hole half the depth of the root ball. Tip the hessian-wrapped ball into the hole, and pile a 150 mm layer of mulch over it. Water the mulch from time to time to prevent the root ball from drying out.

If you plan to replant the tree within a week or so, simply set the root ball in a shady spot and give it a good watering. Do not immerse it in water; the roots will rot if they get too wet.

MULCH

75

The Right Way to Plant a Tree

Trees are common symbols of permanence, yet almost every garden tree is moved at least once in its lifetime—from its birthplace, where it starts life as a seedling, to a new location in a home owner's garden. For this crucial journey, the tree generally takes one of three portable forms: root-balled, container-grown or bare-rooted.

A balled tree, like a tree prepared for transplanting within the garden *(pages 74–75)*, is dug out of the ground and its root ball is tightly wrapped in hessian. If you buy such a tree and do not intend to plant it at once, store it by the method shown on page 75, Step 4. Container-grown trees are seeded and grown in large metal cans or plastic pots. Bare-rooted trees, usually sold by mail-order nurseries, are generally smaller, younger and less expensive than the other two types. But they are more vulnerable to injury as their roots, packed in moist moss peat or sawdust, or wrapped in plastic, are relatively unprotected.

Before buying a young tree in any form, use the species chart on pages 82–83 to find out which species thrive in your area. Test the chemical composition of your soil *(page 33)* and choose a tree that will flourish in it; as a rule, it is always easier to buy a tree that matches your soil than to alter the soil to suit the tree.

At a nursery, look for signs of mishandling, such as scratched bark or broken branches, and of neglect, such as small pale leaves or dry soil. A healthy young tree has dark, glossy, full-sized leaves and a full complement of branches growing from the top two-thirds of its trunk. If you see several unhealthy trees, find another nursery.

If a tree is container-grown, ask the nursery assistant to loosen the container so you can see the roots. They should be thick and many-stranded at the bottom and should not protrude from the top of the soil surface or coil tightly round the root ball—signs of overcrowding. On a balled tree, the root ball should feel firm and solid; crumbling soil indicates that the roots have been torn and may have dried out.

Before planting the tree, create an environment hospitable to it by conditioning the soil you dig out of the planting hole. An organic soil conditioner, such as moss peat or compost, will help sandy soil retain moisture and enable clay-rich earth to drain more efficiently. A newly planted tree which is properly fertilized at the time of planting will not require additional fertilizer for at least another year.

Just after planting a bare-rooted or a balled tree, prune about one-third of the branches; a container-grown tree does not need pruning since it has not lost any of its roots. Wrap the trunk of all new trees with hessian tape, which will expand as the tree grows and protect the tender bark from the sun, from machinery such as a lawn mower and also from gnawing animals. Brace the tree *(Steps 3 to 5, opposite and overleaf, or page 81)*, to steady it and keep the wind from loosening its roots in the new site. Finally, make sure that the tree is watered well; it should receive the equivalent of 25 mm of rainfall a week during the growing season. Always allow the ground around the base of the tree to dry out between each watering.

Planting a Root-Balled Tree

1 **Digging the hole.** Dig a hole twice as wide and one and a half times as deep as the root ball. Put the soil on a sheet of hessian, plastic or canvas to provide a firm surface for mixing in soil conditioners and slow-release fertilizer *(Step 2)*. Aerate the sides of the hole using a fork.

2 Conditioning the soil. Add moss peat, compost or another organic conditioner to the soil removed from the planting hole, mixing the ingredients thoroughly with a spade. Try to confine the mixing job to the sheet—the ingredients will be difficult to handle on grass or ground covers. For loamy soil, add one part moss peat or compost to two parts soil; for clay-rich soil add one part moss peat and one part sand to one part soil. For sandy soil, add one part moss peat to one part soil. Any of the three soil types should also receive an admixture of slow-release fertilizer, in the amount recommended by the fertilizer manufacturer.

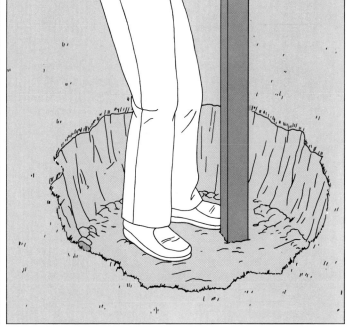

3 Staking the tree. Measure the distance between the top of the root ball and the lowest branch of the tree. Cut a stake from 50 by 50 mm timber a third longer than this measurement, and sharpen one end with a garden knife. Place the tree in the centre of the hole, and push the stake into the ground next to the root ball on the side of the prevailing wind *(above)*.

4 Making a base for the tree. Remove the tree and drive the stake into the ground so that about one-third is below ground level. Fill the planting hole about a third full with the conditioned soil mixture and tamp it down with your feet *(above)*. Repeat the procedure until you have built a firm base round the stake one-third the depth of the hole.

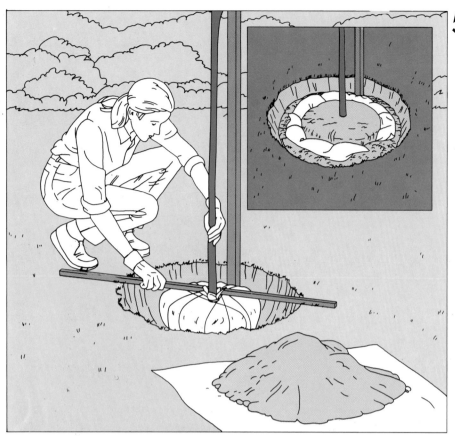

5 **Positioning the tree.** Set the root ball in the centre of the hole, hold the tree trunk vertical and lay a length of wood across the hole to check the level of the ball. The ground at the top of the hole should be even with the top of the root ball or slightly higher, but not above the tree's original soil level as indicated by a darker band of bark at the base of the trunk. If the tree is too high or too low, lift it out and remove or add soil at the bottom of the hole, then reposition the tree. In poor drainage areas, plant the tree a little high.

Add soil mixture to the hole, tamping it down with your foot, until its level is two-thirds the depth of the original hole, then loosen the hessian at the top of the root ball *(inset)* and fill the hole with water. When the water has drained away, fill the hole to ground level with soil mixture and tamp it firmly. Wrap a rubber tree tie round the trunk and secure with two nails to the stake.

TREE TIE

6 **Forming a basin of soil.** To prevent water from draining away from the roots of the trees, build a dyke of soil 50 to 100 mm high round the edge of the planting hole. Fill this basin with water; then, when the water has seeped into the ground, pile a 75 mm-deep mulch of ground bark or bark chips inside the basin and round the trunk.

Planting a Container-Grown Tree

1 **Taking the tree from the container.** Prepare a planting hole by the method shown on pages 76–77. Then, for a metal container, put on heavy leather gloves and cut the container from top to bottom in three or four places with a pair of tin snips. Spread the strips of metal and lift out the root mass without knocking off the soil. A plastic container will usually slide off easily if you rap it gently or squeeze and release its sides; if it does not, cut it with tin snips or heavy scissors.

2 **Arranging the roots.** Unwind the coiled roots around the root mass so they will not strangle each other or grow in circles. Loosen the exposed roots slightly and gently tease apart the root mass with a trowel or spade. Using secateurs, trim off broken roots at the first joint above the break. Set the root mass in the planting hole, spreading out the roots. Build a soil basin round the tree, water the tree well and fill the basin with mulch (*opposite page, Step 6*).

Planting a Bare-Rooted Tree

1 **Positioning the roots.** Dig and prepare a planting hole *(pages 76–77)* about one and a half times as deep as the length of the tree's longest root; make the hole roughly as wide as it is deep. Build up a cone-shaped mound of soil at the centre of the hole. Set the tree in the hole and spread the roots out over the mound. Lay a length of wood across the hole *(page 78, Step 5)* so that the previous soil level mark on the tree trunk is even with or a little higher than ground level. If the mark is below ground level, remove the tree and make the soil mound higher.

2 **Filling the hole around the roots.** Hold the tree in place and scoop the soil mixture into the hole and around the roots. Press the soil down with your hands, working it around the roots to eliminate air pockets. Add soil to two-thirds the depth of the hole, then fill the hole with water. When the water has drained away, fill the hole with soil up to ground level. Build a soil basin and fill it with water, then add mulch *(page 78, Step 6)*.

Caring for the Newly Planted Tree

1 **Pruning the branches.** Immediately after planting a balled or bare-rooted tree, trim away one-third of its branch structure with secateurs. Remove all weak or poorly positioned branches *(page 67)*, but do not cut the main or top leader. Also, do not prune a container-grown tree or any tree that was pruned for you at the nursery.

2 **Wrapping the trunk.** Starting just below the level of the mulch, wind hessian tape up the tree, over-lapping it by 25 mm at each turn. If the tree has branches growing low down, thread the material through them to wrap the trunk up to one-third its height; otherwise, wrap the trunk up to the first branch. Secure the hessian at the top with cotton or hemp twine.

Keep the hessian tape in place for two years. Inspect the twine every few months and loosen it whenever it begins to cut deeply into the tape; the hessian will expand as the tree grows, but the twine must be loosened periodically to prevent it from cutting into the tree's bark.

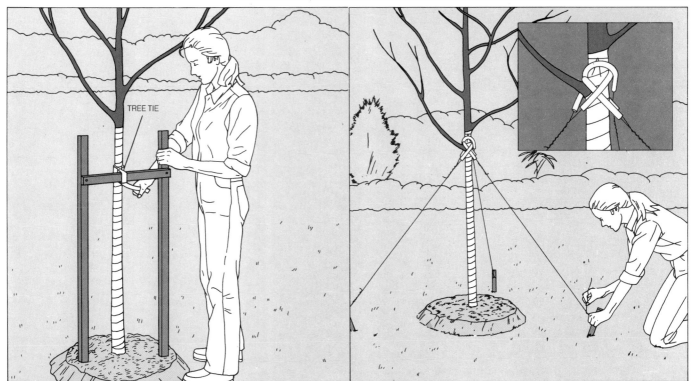

TREE TIE

3 **Bracing the tree.** For a tree with a trunk less than 75 mm thick *(above, left)*, position a pair of 50 by 50 mm posts, 2 metres in length, just in-side the planting hole on either side of the tree, and drive the posts 600 mm into the ground. Nail a 50 by 50 mm piece of timber horizontally be-tween the two posts and attach it to the tree with a rubber tree tie. To brace a tree with a trunk 75 mm or more in diameter *(above, right)*, drive three notched stakes into the ground just outside the planting hole and at equal distances from the trunk and from each other. Thread the end of a guy wire through a 300 mm-long segment of rubber hose, wrap the hose round the trunk above the crotch of a branch and twist the end of the wire back round itself; loop the other end of the wire round the notch in a stake. Add two more wire and hose segments *(inset)*. All the wires should be straight but not taut; leave enough extra length at the stakes so that the wires can be loosened as the tree grows.

A Selection of Garden Trees

Column groups: **Soil** (Moist, Dry) · **Soil pH** (Acid, Alkaline) · **Light** (Light shade, Full sun) · **Height** (To 8 metres, Over 8 metres) · **Growth rate** (Slow, Moderate, Fast) · **Shape** (Columnar, Rounded, Weeping, Spreading, Conical) · **Special traits** (Flowers, Fruit or seeds, Leaf colour, Bark)

Deciduous Trees	Frost-sensitive	Frost-tolerant	Moist	Dry	Acid	Alkaline	Light shade	Full sun	To 8 metres	Over 8 metres	Slow	Moderate	Fast	Columnar	Rounded	Weeping	Spreading	Conical	Flowers	Fruit or seeds	Leaf colour	Bark
ACER CAMPESTRE (field maple)		●					●	●	●		●			●							●	
ACER CIRCINATUM (vine maple)		●	●				●		●			●					●		●	●	●	
ACER GINNALA (Amur maple)		●						●	●			●		●					●	●	●	
ACER GRISEUM (paperbark maple)		●					●	●			●			●							●	●
ACER PALMATUM (Japanese maple)		●	●				●		●		●			●							●	
ACER PLATANOIDES (Norway maple)		●	●				●	●		●		●		●							●	
AESCULUS HIPPOCASTANUM (horse chestnut)		●	●					●		●	●						●		●	●		
AESCULUS INDICA (Indian horse chestnut)		●	●					●		●		●					●		●	●		
AILANTHUS ALTISSIMA (tree of heaven)		●					●	●		●			●		●		●			●		
AMELANCHIER GRANDIFLORA (snowy mespilus)		●	●					●				●		●					●			
ARALIA ELATA (Japanese angelica tree)		●					●	●	●			●		●					●			
BETULA PENDULA (silver birch)		●	●					●		●		●				●		●			●	●
CARPINUS BETULUS (common hornbeam)		●						●	●	●				●				●			●	
CASTANEA MOLLISSIMA (Chinese chestnut)		●		●				●	●								●		●	●	●	
CATALPA BIGNONIOIDES (Indian bean tree)		●						●	●			●		●					●			
CERCIS SILIQUASTRUM (Eastern Judas tree)		●	●				●	●			●			●					●	●	●	
CORNUS FLORIDA (flowering dogwood)		●	●		●			●	●		●				●	●	●		●	●	●	
CORNUS KOUSA (Kousa dogwood)		●	●		●			●	●		●						●		●	●	●	
CRATAEGUS MONOGYNA (hawthorn)		●					●	●			●			●					●	●	●	
CRATAEGUS PHAENOPYRUM (Washington hawthorn)		●						●	●	●							●		●	●	●	
DAVIDIA INVOLUCRATA (handkerchief tree)		●	●					●	●		●			●					●			
DELONIX REGIA (royal poinciana)	●							●	●			●					●		●		●	
ELAEAGNUS ANGUSTIFOLIA (oleaster)		●					●	●	●			●		●					●	●	●	●
FRAXINUS ORNUS (manna ash)		●						●				●		●					●			
FRAXINUS OXYCARPA (ash)		●			●	●		●				●		●							●	
FRAXINUS VELUTINA (Arizona ash)		●		●		●		●				●					●				●	
GINKGO BILOBA (maidenhair tree)		●			●		●	●				●		●						●	●	
GLEDITSIA TRIACANTHOS (honey locust)		●	●	●				●		●		●		●			●	●			●	
HALESIA CAROLINA (silver bell tree)		●						●	●			●	●						●		●	
JACARANDA ACUTIFOLIA (sharp-leaved jacaranda)	●			●				●	●			●					●		●		●	
JUGLANS NIGRA (black walnut)			●					●	●					●						●		
KOELREUTERIA PANICULATA (golden-rain tree)		●			●			●	●			●							●			
LABURNUM ANAGYROIDES (common laburnum)		●	●				●				●			●		●			●	●		
LABURNUM x WATERERI (Waterer laburnum)		●	●			●	●				●			●					●			
LIQUIDAMBAR STYRACIFLUA (sweet gum)		●	●		●	●					●							●	●	●	●	
MAGNOLIA x SOULANGIANA (saucer magnolia)		●	●		●				●		●						●		●	●	●	●
MALUS FLORIBUNDA (Japanese crab apple)		●	●		●		●	●			●				●				●	●	●	
MALUS 'RED JADE' (red-jade crab apple)		●	●		●		●	●				●				●			●	●	●	
MALUS TSCHONOSKII (Tschonoskii crab apple)		●	●		●			●		●		●						●		●		
MALUS ZUMI CALOCARPA (Zumi crab apple)		●	●		●		●	●				●			●				●	●	●	
OXYDENDRUM ARBOREUM (sorrel tree)		●	●		●		●	●		●	●				●				●	●	●	
PAULOWNIA TOMENTOSA (Paulownia)	●			●	●	●		●				●		●					●	●		
PISTACIA CHINENSIS (Chinese pistachio)	●					●		●				●		●					●	●		

Choosing a suitable tree. This chart lists 80 small and medium-sized ornamental trees suitable for a garden or patio; of these, 54 are deciduous trees, 12 are narrow-leaved evergreens and 14 are broad-leaved evergreens. The first column gives the trees' Latin names in alphabetical order, followed by their common English names in brackets. The second and third columns indicate each tree's tolerance of frost. Special requirements for level of moisture, type of soil and intensity of light are indicated by dots; in each of these categories, trees without any distinct preferences are not marked by dots. In the column for Growth rate, a slow-growing tree is one that adds less than 300 mm to its height annually; a moderate

Species	Frost-sensitive	Frost-tolerant	Moist	Dry	Acid	Alkaline	Light shade	Full sun	To 8 metres	Over 8 metres	Slow	Moderate	Fast	Columnar	Rounded	Weeping	Spreading	Conical	Flowers	Fruit or seeds	Leaf colour	Bark
PRUNUS AVIUM 'PLENA' (double-flowered mazzard cherry)		●					●		●			●					●		●			
PRUNUS CERASIFERA 'ATROPURPUREA' (Pissard cherry plum)		●					●	●				●			●				●	●	●	
PRUNUS SERRULA (paperbark cherry)		●					●	●				●			●				●	●		●
PRUNUS SUBHIRTELLA (spring cherry)		●					●	●				●				●			●			
PRUNUS x YEDOENSIS (Yoshino cherry)		●						●	●			●					●		●			
PYRUS CALLERYANA 'BRADFORD' (Bradford pear)		●						●		●	●							●	●	●	●	
QUERCUS ROBUR (common oak)		●			●			●		●	●				●					●		
ROBINIA PSEUDOACACIA (locust or false acacia)		●		●		●		●		●		●		●					●	●		
SORBUS AUCUPARIA (European mountain ash)		●						●		●		●					●		●	●	●	
STYRAX JAPONICA (Japanese snowbell)	●	●						●	●								●		●		●	
SYRINGA RETICULATA (Japanese tree lilac)	●	●					●	●			●						●		●			

Narrow-Leaved Evergreens

Species	Frost-sensitive	Frost-tolerant	Moist	Dry	Acid	Alkaline	Light shade	Full sun	To 8 metres	Over 8 metres	Slow	Moderate	Fast	Columnar	Rounded	Weeping	Spreading	Conical	Flowers	Fruit or seeds	Leaf colour	Bark
CHAMAECYPARIS LAWSONIANA (Lawson cypress)	●	●					●		●		●							●				
CRYPTOMERIA JAPONICA (Japanese cedar)	●	●		●			●		●			●						●	●	●	●	
CUNNINGHAMIA LANCEOLATA (China fir)	●			●				●				●						●	●	●	●	
CUPRESSUS SEMPERVIRENS 'STRICTA' (Italian cypress)	●		●				●		●		●	●							●	●		
JUNIPERUS CHINENSIS 'COLUMNARIS' (blue column juniper)		●	●				●	●			●			●							●	
LIBOCEDRUS DECURRENS (California incense cedar)	●	●						●		●		●		●					●		●	
PICEA OMORIKA (Serbian spruce)		●					●			●	●							●	●			
PINUS DENSIFLORA 'UMBRACULIFERA' (Japanese red pine)		●	●				●	●	●								●		●		●	
PINUS THUNBERGII (Japanese black pine)		●	●				●		●			●					●	●	●			
PODOCARPUS MACROPHYLLUS (Chinese yew)	●	●			●		●			●		●		●							●	
SCIADOPITYS VERTICILLATA (Japanese umbrella pine)	●	●		●			●	●		●								●	●			
TAXUS BACCATA 'FASTIGIATA' (Irish yew)		●		●				●	●		●			●					●	●		

Broad-Leaved Evergreens

Species	Frost-sensitive	Frost-tolerant	Moist	Dry	Acid	Alkaline	Light shade	Full sun	To 8 metres	Over 8 metres	Slow	Moderate	Fast	Columnar	Rounded	Weeping	Spreading	Conical	Flowers	Fruit or seeds	Leaf colour	Bark
ACACIA DEALBATA (silver wattle)	●			●				●					●				●				●	
CINNAMOMUM CAMPHORA (camphor tree)	●							●		●	●				●				●	●	●	
CITRUS SINENSIS (sweet orange)	●		●				●	●			●			●					●	●		
ERIOBOTRYA JAPONICA (loquat)	●		●					●				●			●				●	●		
EUCALYPTUS GUNNII (cider gum)	●						●		●			●					●				●	●
ILEX AQUIFOLIUM (English holly)		●			●		●		●	●	●			●					●	●	●	
LAURUS NOBILIS (bay laurel)	●							●	●		●							●	●			
NERIUM OLEANDER (oleander)	●		●				●	●				●		●					●			
OLEA EUROPAEA (common olive)	●			●			●	●				●		●					●	●		●
OSMANTHUS HETEROPHYLLUS (holly osmanthus)		●		●		●		●				●		●					●			
PHOTINIA x FRASERI (Fraser photinia)		●						●		●						●			●	●	●	
QUERCUS ILEX (holm oak)		●	●					●	●		●			●							●	
SCHINUS MOLLE (California pepper tree)	●						●	●		●		●				●			●	●		
ULMUS PARVIFOLIA (Chinese elm)		●		●				●	●			●				●					●	

growth rate is between 300 and 600 mm a year; fast growth is 900 mm or more a year. Tree shapes can sometimes vary within a single species; in the Shape column, each variation is indicated by a dot. Variation is much wider and more common in the column for Special traits, for instance striking leaf colour or unusual bark, which give a tree a distinctive appearance; here, too, multiple dots may appear on the chart, indicating variations within a species.

Shrubs: Beautiful, Versatile, Easy to Maintain

Of all the elements in a landscape, shrubs are surely the most versatile. They serve as backgrounds for gardens, low dividers to separate the garden into different areas, and thick, tall screens for privacy. They are equally diverse in their decorative effects, ranging from bursts of floral brilliance to perennially green displays; and with some training or trimming, they can add a variety of shapes and textures to the garden.

Fortunately, these all-purpose plants are among the easiest to care for. A simple programme of feeding, watering, weeding, pruning and, in certain climates, protecting the shrubs from cold weather in winter, will make shrubs luxuriant during the growing season and keep them healthy throughout the year.

Throughout the summer, give them a long, slow watering every two weeks—every seven to 10 days during dry spells. Add fertilizer to the beds just before or during spring growth, but not in midsummer or late summer; the nutrients stimulate new growth that will not have time to harden before winter.

Add mulch or compost to the beds of all shrubs, not only to provide nutrients, but also to keep the soil cool in summer and warm in winter, and to inhibit weed growth. You can buy bark chippings or other organic mulch by the bag at garden centres; alternatively, you can use pine needles or leaves from the garden and organic waste from the kitchen to create a compost heap of your own *(page 35)*. Whatever you choose, simply spread it in a 50 to 75 mm layer round each plant and renew it in spring and autumn.

If mulch or compost alone fails to control weeds, you must either pull them by hand or eliminate them with chemical weed killers before they rob plants of nutrients.

A local garden centre or nursery can tell you which chemicals work best against the weeds in your area.

Pruning is the most time-consuming task in shrub care, but few tasks are more important. Pruning eliminates damaged and diseased wood that can imperil a plant's health, sometimes in unexpected ways. Crossing branches, for instance, can rub against each other, leaving the plant vulnerable to infection; such branches, along with all damaged, dead or diseased wood, should be cut off. Pruning also encourages new growth and—especially in roses—boosts flower, fruit and foliage production by reducing the number of limbs that must be sustained by the roots and circulatory system. Finally, pruning keeps the shrub within bounds and shapes it.

Four simple hand tools will enable you to meet these objectives efficiently and easily. You will need a pair of secateurs, to clip small branches that are within easy reach; lopping shears, to remove larger branches above your head; hedge clippers, to snip off leaves and twigs when you are shaping a bush or hedge; and a small pruning saw, to cut stems which are too thick for the lighter hand tools.

The various species of shrubs require different degrees of pruning and at different times of the year. If you are in any doubt about what to do for a particular shrub, consult a gardening centre or pruning manual. In general, deciduous shrubs that flower on old wood in the spring and early summer should be pruned immediately after flowering. But summer and early autumn-flowering shrubs, which bloom on the current year's growth, are pruned in early spring before the buds form.

Spring is a good time to remove any parts of a shrub that have been damaged

by winter weather and to do some light shaping and trimming. To rejuvenate older plants, more drastic measures may be needed. Each year cut back some of the old stems to within 50 to 100 mm of the ground, forcing new stems to develop.

As winter approaches, some shrubs may need protection from wind, cold and snow. To determine which of your plants to protect, check the chart on pages 94–95. A local nursery can advise about specific shrubs; a local gardening club may also be a good source of information about plants that need help to get through the winter.

Some methods of protecting shrubs are shown on page 89. For the best results, use these methods between the first frost of autumn and the first hard freeze of winter. In sudden spells of severe cold you may also want to protect plants temporarily. Wrap them in hessian or even throw a blanket over them, but remove such makeshift shields as soon as the cold snap abates.

Heavy, wet snow is especially damaging to evergreen shrubs. After a fall of snow, knock the snow off with a broom or a stick, or shake the shrub gently to dislodge the snow. Take care not to snap the branches, which may be brittle with the cold.

Winter damage to broad-leaved evergreens frequently results from leaf transpiration, the technical term for water loss by evaporation. To minimize such damage, thoroughly soak the ground around the plants in the autumn, before the first hard freeze; then place heavy mulch, such as a mixture of leaves and straw, round the stem over the tops of the roots, keeping the mulch in place with a cylinder of wire. A commercial antitranspirant—a waxy substance that can be sprayed on to the shrub periodically during the winter—will also help to hold moisture in the leaves.

Using Shrubs in a Landscape

A variety of roles. Used alone or in combination, shrubs create an extraordinary range of effects. Planted close together, a number of shrubs of the same species form a hedge to provide a screen against a neighbour or the street. A hedge can be a background for gardens or sculpture, or define an area for play or outdoor living. A border, like a hedge but with a variety of different shrub species, can be used in the same ways; but it is less effective as a background because of its diverse and distracting colours and textures.

In the language of landscape architecture, a group is an island of plants rising above the ground. In the example shown here, consisting of several shrubs round a tree, the shrubs offset the vertical effect of the tree; other examples might be combinations of variously sized and coloured shrubs chosen for their intrinsic beauty. A specimen—a single plant with a noteworthy quality, such as a profusion of flowers, imposing size or a particularly pleasing shape—is usually placed where it can be seen from inside the house as well as from the garden. An accent plant, for example, can be the focal point of a border or group, or it can add a graceful note at a corner of the house or beside the front door.

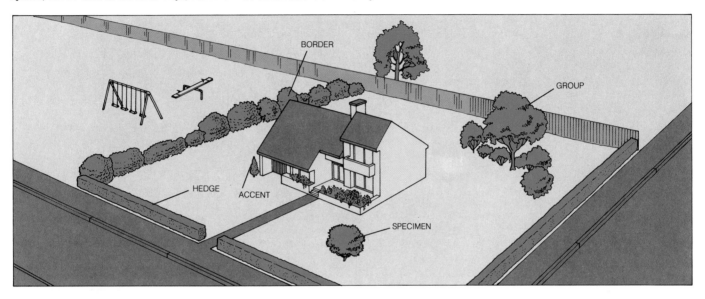

Routine Care to Keep Shrubs Healthy

Stirring up the soil. Before weeding a shrub bed, cultivate the soil with a hoe to loosen weeds and break up compacted soil. Push the blade of the hoe *(inset)* into the ground, keeping it parallel to the soil, then work the blade forwards and backwards at a depth of about 25 to 50 mm; do not work so deeply that you catch roots. After weeding, use the hoe again to smooth out the soil.

Getting water to the roots. Give large plants a long, slow soaking, keeping the water aimed at the roots. For one common soaking method, attach the hose end to a sprinkler extension, a wand-like device that breaks up the stream of water to shower the bed gently *(below, left)*. Al-ternatively—particularly for hedges, groups or young plants—you can use a perforated hose *(below, right)*. This is a length of hose pierced by tiny holes, from which water either seeps or sprinkles according to the pressure. Perforated hoses are available in lengths of 7.5 metres.

PERFORATED HOSE

Spreading mulch. To keep shrub roots from drying in the summer sun and to prevent deep frost penetration in the winter, spread an even layer of mulch on the bed. If you use dense material, such as bark chips or ground bark, spread the mulch about 50 mm deep. If you use a looser material, such as pine needles or oak leaves, make the layer about 75 mm thick. Cover the entire shrub basin, but do not pack the material tightly round the plant stems; moisture in the mulch could produce rot. Do not put mulch on dry soil; it would slow the passage of rainwater to the root system.

Pruning: the Kindest Cuts of All

Trimming for shape. Grasp a branch just below a bud and set the cutting blade of a pair of seca-teurs between 3 and 6 mm above the bud. Hold-ing the secateurs at a 45-degree angle slanting away from the bud, sever the branch with a smooth, firm squeeze of the handles. To ensure that new branches grow away from the main trunk, as indicated by the dotted lines in this ex-ample, make each cut at a lateral bud—that is, a bud pointing outwards from the side of a shoot.

Trimming hedges. To speed the trimming of a formal hedge, use an electric or battery-operated trimmer. Stretch a level string tightly between posts at the ends of the hedge to indicate the level of the cut. Then hold the trimmer flat at the level of the string and draw it across the hedge top; do not poke the tip of the trimmer into the hedge. As an alternative, use hedge clippers *(inset)*.

If any long shoots are growing into a gap in the hedge, cut the shoots back with secateurs to stimulate thick growth that will fill the hole.

Shape an informal, relatively irregular hedge as you would a shrub, using secateurs and trying to create a natural, feathery appearance; take particular care to prune out any branches that have grown faster than the others.

Trim both formal and informal hedges narrower at the top than at the bottom, to permit sunlight to reach the base of the hedge. After trimming a hedge, shake it to dislodge the clippings, then rake the clippings away.

Removing damaged wood. Use secateurs to cut away dead, broken or diseased branches. Always cut right back to healthy wood—either at a point just above a lateral bud or, as in the example on the left, flush with the nearest healthy stem.

Thinning for health and light. Remove all weak, misshapen or crossing stems, using secateurs, lopping shears *(right)* or a small curved saw, according to the thickness of the wood. Then cut up to one-third of the healthy stems from the centre of the shrub to allow light to reach the interior foliage. In both stages of the job, remove entire branches at a main stem or cut through a main stem at ground level.

Pruning Rose Bushes

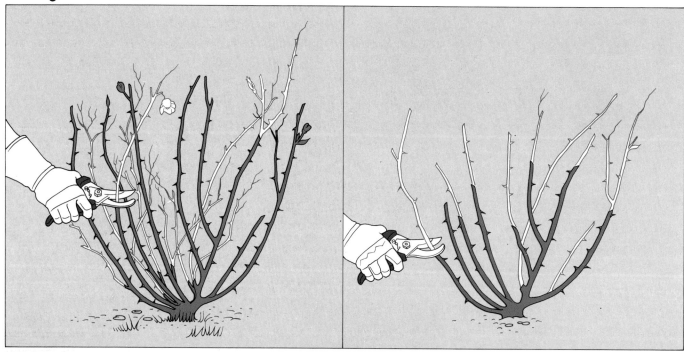

Cutting for more and better blossoms. Rose bushes need regular and extensive pruning to produce strong shoots and large flowers. In the autumn, cut back every branch by a third of its length; cut away dead wood, small shoots and crossing branches, and thin the interior branches. After this pruning, the bush should be about two-thirds of its original size, as indicated by the area shown in solid colour *(above, left)*.

In the spring, remove any weak, stringy branches and frost-damaged wood, and cut back all the main branches to sound stems at least 10 mm thick. This spring pruning should leave a low, bowl-shaped plant with several main stems, as shown in solid colour *(above, right)*.

During the growing season, prune roses as you would any other shrub, cutting out dead and damaged wood and small branches. Suckers should be traced back to the point of growth and cut or pulled off.

Helping Shrubs to Get Through the Winter

Protecting a shrub from wind and snow. To protect a low-growing shrub, such as heather, cover the plant with branches and trimmings from needle-bearing evergreens *(below, left)*, such as a discarded Christmas tree.

For medium-height shrubs that are exposed to the full force of the wind, build a shelter of stakes and hessian to the full height of the shrub *(below, centre)*. First, drive several stakes in a tight circle all round the plant, then staple the hessian to the stakes; the hessian should hug the branches, compressing them slightly. Tie needled evergreens with cord or twine to prevent heavy, wet snow from settling on the branches and breaking them. Starting at the bottom, wrap the cord round the shrub tightly enough to hold the branches upright *(below, right)*. Brush off any snow that settles after heavy falls.

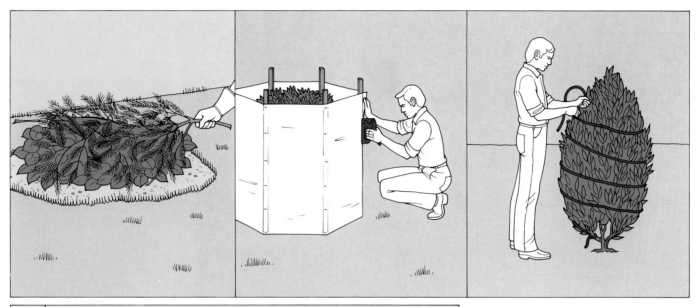

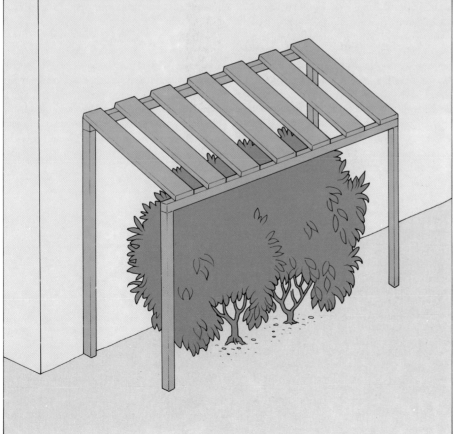

A shield for shrubs beneath an eave. A sloping shelter on a frame of 75 by 50 mm supports prevents the snow that slides off a roof from damaging shrubs along a house wall. Drive one pair of 75 by 50 mm posts, about 300 mm taller than the shrubs, into the ground behind the shrubs at the house wall. Put up a second, shorter pair in front of the shrubs. Connect the tops of each pair crosswise with two more 75 by 50 mm posts, and roof the structure with scrap boards spaced from 100 to 150 mm apart.

Putting Plants in New Places

Because they grow quickly and can be set in place for immediate effect, transplanted or newly planted shrubs are ideal for making rapid changes in a landscape. For the most part, they are planted in much the same way as trees *(pages 76–81)*, although you can save time when planting a hedge by digging a trench and setting in all the plants at once. The general rule, which applies to nearly every hedge species, is to space new shrubs at intervals of 1 metre; slow-growing shrubs, such as hollies, or those with a strongly upright form, such as yews, can be planted closer together. When buying shrubs for a hedge, get a few extra plants and grow them elsewhere in the garden so that you will have a replacement on hand if a shrub in the hedge dies.

New shrubs are obtainable from a variety of sources. The most convenient, though also the most expensive, is a nursery. Choose a reputable one, which sells healthy shrubs acclimatized to your region, and examine the shrubs carefully. They will come in one of three ways: with the roots in a ball of soil wrapped in hessian, with the roots bare, or rooted in a large plastic container. Check a root-balled plant to see that the ball is intact, free of weeds and moist. Bare roots should be creamy white, not dark and foul-smelling. On any new shrub the leaves should be shiny and full, and the main stem should be centred above the root system; a lopsided stem will produce a lopsided top and a weak root system.

Transplanting shrubs is harder work than buying a new plant from a nursery or garden centre, but the transplanted shrub costs nothing at all, and moving a shrub away from a location can sometimes be as desirable as adding one elsewhere. Transplanting is best done in early spring or autumn; first, give the shrub a generous watering two days before the move—in order to soften the soil round the roots—and tie up the branches with twine.

Propagating new plants from existing ones is a third source of shrubs. Although propagating, like transplanting, is free—or better than free, since you get two or more plants for the price of one—a year or more may pass before you get the plant you want. Choose the parent plant with care; the new shrub will be an exact duplicate of the one from which it is propagated, with all of the characteristics, both good and bad, of its parent. Azaleas, roses and many more species of shrub can be propagated by the cutting method shown on page 56. For others, such as forsythia or rhododendrons, use the method called ground layering which is shown on page 93. If you are in doubt about the appropriate method for propagating a particular species of shrub, ask your local nursery for advice.

Whether you are planting or transplanting, have the hole ready for the shrub in advance. If it is not possible to plant the shrub immediately, store it in a cool, shady place and keep the roots moist. Do not store a bare-rooted shrub in this way for more than a week; if you have to wait longer, lay the shrub in a trench, cover its roots with soil and keep it watered until you are ready to plant it.

Discarding an Unwanted Shrub

1 **Digging out the roots.** Cut off most of the shrub's branches with secateurs, but leave the main stem or a small clump of main stems 600 to 900 mm long to serve as a handle. Use a mattock to cut a circle about 600 mm in diameter round the shrub and down through the root system, then undercut the shrub with a spade and pull the plant out by the stems. Proceed immediately to Step 2.

2 Refilling the hole. Hold the root ball of the shrub over the hole and, with a fork or other sharp tool, scrape all of the soil from the roots back into the hole. Fill the hole with additional soil and tamp it down, then add still more soil to form a loose mound about 100 to 150 mm high; the mound will settle naturally in two to three months, leaving the area level.

Transplanting a Shrub

1 Defining the digging area. Using a spade, mark a circle round the shrub to be transplanted directly under the outer edge of the foliage; then, with the blade facing towards the plant, plunge the spade 200 to 220 mm deep into the soil along the outline of the circle. In the same way, mark and cut a second circle which is wider than the first by the width of the spade blade.

2 Cutting out the root ball. Dig out the soil between the two circles to the level of the shrub's major roots, generally about 450 mm down. Working around the root ball from different directions, undercut the shrub with the spade; then carefully scratch and chop the soil beneath the shrub until the ball comes loose. A small shrub can be removed now; for a larger shrub, go on to Step 3.

3 Wrapping the root ball. When the roots are free, push against one side of the root ball to tip the shrub, and stuff several folds of hessian into the gap *(below, left)*. Let the ball roll back, and tip it in the opposite direction; then grasp the hessian and pull it under the ball *(below, right)*. Lift the edges of the hessian and tie them tightly round the stem of the shrub with some twine.

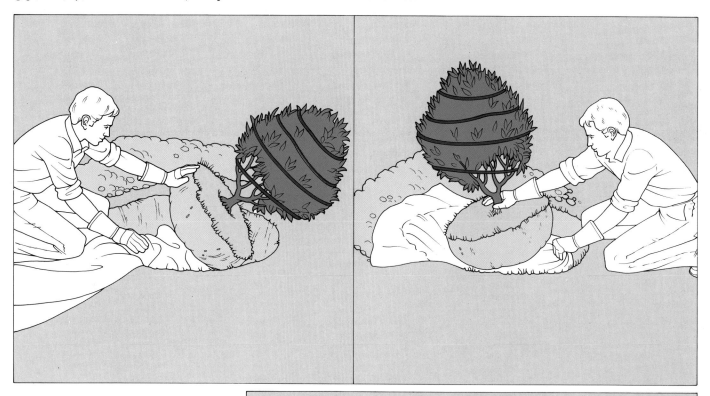

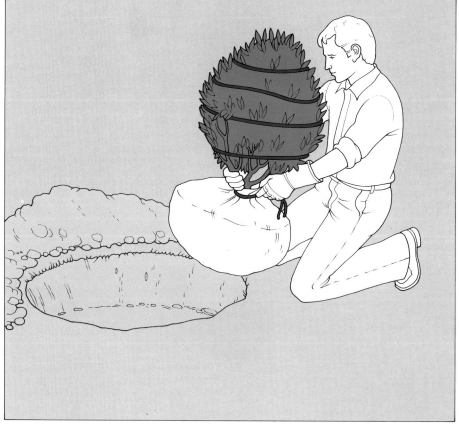

4 Pulling out the shrub. Grasp the hessian at the top of the root ball and lift the shrub out of the hole; you may need a helper for medium or large-sized shrubs. Set the shrub on a sheet of plastic or hardboard, and slide the sheet along the ground to the desired location. Following the steps shown on pages 76–78, plant the shrub; to allow for settling, set the roots 25 to 50 mm shallower than their original depth.

Prune the transplanted shrub to compensate for roots lost during digging; also remove any broken branches and shape the plant.

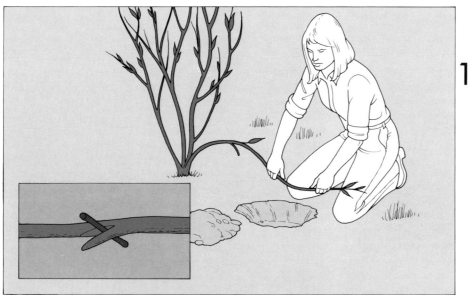

Propagating Shrubs by Layering

1 Wounding the branch. In early spring, bend a healthy lower branch of the plant to be propagated until it touches the ground about 300 mm from its tip. Dig a dish-shaped hole 150 mm deep at that position.

Bend the branch into the hole. At the point in the branch that touches the centre of the hole, cut diagonally half way through the branch from below, using a pruning knife or a sharp pocket knife, and wedge the wound open with a pebble or a matchstick *(inset)*. Sprinkle the open wound with rooting powder, a synthetic hormone that is available at nurseries and garden centres.

2 Anchoring the branch. Pour a mixture of equal parts of topsoil, moss peat and sand into the hole to a depth of 50 mm. Bend the branch back into the hole with the wound facing downwards, and anchor the branch in position with two crossed sticks; beyond the sticks, bend the branch up so that it rises about 150 mm above ground level. Cover the anchored branch and fill the hole with more of the soil mix. Water the soil mix thoroughly and place a rock on top of the crossed sticks to hold them in place.

3 Separating the new shrub. After about a year, dig out the buried branch and gently push away some soil to check for new roots. If the wound has produced three to five good roots, sever the branch to free the new root ball from the main plant *(left)*. If the wound has not yet produced enough new roots, re-bury the branch until autumn and check again.

Once a satisfactory set of roots has been produced, push gently on the root ball to slant the roots away from the tip of the branch, then plant the propagated shrub as you would any other shrub. Tilt the ball as you set it into the hole, pointing the branch tip upwards.

A Selection of Garden Shrubs

Flowering

Name	Frost-sensitive	Frost-tolerant	Hedge	Ground cover	Moist	Dry	Acid	Sun	Shade	Under 1 metre	1 to 2 metres	Over 2 metres	White	Yellow-orange	Pink-red	Blue-purple	Spring	Summer	Autumn	Fruit	Foliage	Fragrance
	Uses				Soil			Light		Height			Flower colour				Flower season			Special traits		
AESCULUS PARVIFLORA (**dwarf horse chestnut, bottle-brush buckeye**)		●									●	●	●					●			●	
ARONIA ARBUTIFLORA (**brilliant chokeberry**)		●									●	●	●		●					●	●	
ARONIA MELANOCARPA (**black chokeberry**)		●						●				●	●		●					●	●	
BERBERIS DARWINII (**Darwin barberry**)	●		●								●			●			●			●		
BERBERIS THUNBERGII (**Japanese barberry**)	●		●								●			●			●			●		
BUDDLEIA ALTERNIFOLIA (**buddleia**)		●					●				●				●	●	●				●	●
CALYCANTHUS FLORIDUS (**Carolina allspice**)		●		●					●			●			●		●				●	●
CHAENOMELES HYBRIDS (**hybrid flowering quince**)	●		●					●			●		●		●		●			●		
CLETHRA ALNIFOLIA (**sweet pepper bush**)		●		●	●			●			●		●					●			●	●
CORNUS MAS (**cornelian cherry**)		●									●	●		●			●			●		
CORYLOPSIS GLABRESCENS (**fragrant winter hazel**)		●		●	●						●	●		●			●				●	●
CORYLUS AVELLANA 'CONTORTA' (**corkscrew hazel**)		●									●	●		●			●				●	
COTONEASTER ADPRESSUS (**cotoneaster**)		●			●			●					●					●		●	●	
COTONEASTER HORIZONTALIS (**horizontal cotoneaster**)		●		●	●			●					●	●				●		●	●	
COTONEASTER RACEMIFLORUS (**Sungari cotoneaster**)		●			●						●	●						●		●	●	
CYTISUS HYBRIDS (**hybrid broom**)		●			●			●	●	●	●		●	●	●	●	●					●
DAPHNE MEZEREUM (**mezereon**)		●						●			●			●		●	●			●		
DEUTZIA GRACILIS (**slender deutzia**)	●		●						●		●					●		●				
ELAEAGNUS ANGUSTIFOLIA (**oleaster**)	●		●					●			●	●		●				●		●	●	●
ENKIANTHUS CAMPANULATUS (**red vein enkianthus**)		●		●	●						●	●		●			●				●	
EXOCHORDA RACEMOSA (**common pearlbush**)		●						●			●	●	●				●					
FORSYTHIA X INTERMEDIA (**forsythia**)	●		●								●			●			●					
HAMAMELIS MOLLIS (**Chinese witch hazel**)		●		●							●			●			●				●	●
HYDRANGEA PANICULATA (**hydrangea paniculata**)		●		●							●	●	●					●	●			
JASMINUM NUDIFLORUM (**winter jasmine**)		●						●			●			●			●					
KERRIA JAPONICA (**kerria**)	●								●			●		●			●	●	●		●	
KOLKWITZIA AMABILIS (**beauty bush**)		●						●			●				●		●			●	●	
LAGERSTROEMIA INDICA (**crape myrtle**)	●			●				●			●	●	●	●			●				●	
LIGUSTRUM OBTUSIFOLIUM (**Regel privet**)	●		●						●		●						●			●		
LIGUSTRUM OVALIFOLIUM, 'AUREUM' (**golden privet**)	●		●								●	●					●			●	●	
LONICERA FRAGRANTISSIMA (**winter honeysuckle**)		●							●		●				●		●			●		●
LONICERA MAACKII (**Amur honeysuckle**)		●									●	●	●				●			●		
LONICERA TATARICA (**Tartarian honeysuckle**)		●									●	●			●		●			●		
PHILADELPHUS x LEMOINEI (**mock orange**)		●							●		●		●					●				●
PHOTINIA VILLOSA (**oriental photinia**)		●				●					●	●	●				●			●	●	
POTENTILLA FRUTICOSA (**cinquefoil**)		●					●			●	●	●		●				●	●			
PRUNUS BESSEYI (**rocky mountain cherry**)	●		●					●			●		●				●			●		
PRUNUS MARITIMA (**beach plum**)		●						●			●		●				●			●		
PRUNUS TRILOBA (**flowering almond**)		●						●				●			●		●			●	●	
RHODODENDRON CALENDULACEUM (**flame azalea**)		●		●	●						●			●	●		●					
RHODODENDRON, EXBURY HYBRIDS (**hybrid azalea**)		●		●	●		●				●		●	●	●		●				●	
RHODODENDRON LUTESCENS (**azalea**)		●		●	●						●			●			●					
ROBINIA HISPIDA (**rose acacia**)		●	●					●			●				●		●	●				
ROSA RUGOSA (**Japanese rose**)		●						●			●		●		●		●	●	●	●	●	●
SALIX DISCOLOR (**pussy willow**)		●		●				●			●	●		●			●					
SORBARIA SORBIFOLIA (**Ural false spiraea**)		●		●							●	●	●					●				
SPIRAEA JAPONICA 'ANTHONY WATERER' (**spiraea 'Anthony Waterer'**)		●						●			●				●			●			●	

	Frost-sensitive	Frost-tolerant	Hedge	Ground cover	Moist	Dry	Acid	Sun	Shade	Under 1 metre	1 to 2 metres	Over 2 metres	White	Yellow-orange	Pink-red	Blue-purple	Spring	Summer	Autumn	Fruit	Foliage	Fragrance
SPIRAEA PRUNIFOLIA (**bridal wreath spiraea**)	●	●									●	●	●				●				●	
SYMPHORICARPOS ALBUS (**snowberry**)	●	●							●						●			●		●		
SYRINGA VULGARIS (**common lilac**)	●										●	●	●		●	●	●					●
TAMARIX RAMOSISSIMA (**five-stamened tamarisk**)	●					●					●				●			●			●	
VIBURNUM X CARLCEPHALUM (**fragrant snowball viburnum**)	●	●									●	●	●				●			●	●	●
VIBURNUM PLICATUM 'MARIESII' (**Marie's doublefile viburnum**)	●	●									●	●	●				●			●	●	
VIBURNUM SIEBOLDII (**Siebold viburnum**)	●										●	●	●				●			●	●	
WEIGELA HYBRIDS (**hybrid weigela**)	●									●	●		●		●	●	●					

Choosing a flowering shrub. This chart, which begins on the opposite page, lists 55 flowering shrubs in alphabetical order by their botanical Latin names, followed by their common English names. To find the characteristics of each shrub, follow the lines across the page to the dots underneath the headings.

Some of the plants are listed without dots in some categories. Under the column for Uses, dots are entered only for plants which are specialized as hedges or ground covers. In the Soil and Light columns, a dot indicates a strong preference or a particular requirement; the absence of dots indicates that a plant can adapt to a variety of different soil and light conditions.

Evergreen

	Frost-sensitive	Frost-tolerant	Lawn specimen	Hedge	Screen	Ground cover	Fruits or berries	Moist	Dry	Acid	Alkaline	Under 300 mm	To 1 metre	1 to 2 metres	To 3 metres	White	Yellow-orange	Pink-red	Green	Dark green	Yellow-green	Blue-green
ARCTOSTAPHYLOS UVA-URSI (**bearberry**)		●				●	●		●	●		●						●		●		
BUXUS SEMPERVIRENS 'SUFFRUTICOSA' (**edging box**)		●	●	●				●					●									●
CAMELLIA JAPONICA (**common camellia**)	●		●	●				●		●				●	●	●		●		●		
CHAMAECYPARIS OBTUSA 'NANA' (**Hinoki cypress**)		●	●					●					●							●		
CHAMAECYPARIS PISIFERA 'FILIFERA NANA' (**Sawara cypress**)		●			●	●		●			●										●	
ILEX CORNUTA (**horned holly**)		●		●			●	●							●					●		
ILEX CRENATA (**Japanese holly**)		●		●			●	●						●						●		
ILEX OPACA (**American holly**)		●	●				●	●							●				●			
JUNIPERUS CHINENSIS 'AUREA' (**golden juniper**)		●	●		●										●						●	
JUNIPERUS HORIZONTALIS (**creeping juniper**)		●				●					●											●
JUNIPERUS SABINA (**Savin juniper**)		●				●							●									●
KALMIA LATIFOLIA (**mountain laurel**)		●	●				●			●				●				●	●			
LEPTOSPERUM SCOPARIUM (**tea tree**)	●		●							●				●		●	●			●		
LIGUSTRUM JAPONICUM (**Japanese privet**)		●		●											●	●	●			●		
MAHONIA AQUIFOLIUM (**Oregon grape**)		●					●						●				●		●			
NANDINA DOMESTICA (**nandina**)	●					●	●						●						●			
PICEA GLAUCA 'CONICA' (**dwarf Alberta spruce**)		●	●	●	●									●						●		
PINUS MUGO (**mountain pine**)		●	●	●	●								●							●		
PYRACANTHA COCCINEA (**firethorn**)		●		●			●								●	●	●			●		
RHODODENDRON KAEMPFERI (**Kaempferi hybrid azalea**)	●	●				●				●			●					●		●		
TAXUS BACCATA 'REPANDENS' (**spreading English yew**)		●	●	●						●			●							●		

Choosing an evergreen shrub. This chart lists 21 evergreen shrubs by their botanical Latin names, then by their common English names. The lack of colour indication means that the species does not bloom conspicuously. Otherwise the dotting system follows that of the chart on flowering shrubs.

Brightening a Landscape with Beds of Flowers

Unlike lawns, trees and shrubs, which enhance a landscape relatively permanently, flowers are mere grace notes—short-lived splashes of colour that come and go faster than the seasons. But whatever the character of a garden, there is room for the colour and variety of flowers. They can be tucked along the wall of a house, massed in a bed or displayed in a thick, bright border along the edge of a lawn or path.

When choosing flowers for your own garden, consider their colour, height, flower size, length of life and time of blooming. Tall flowers should be planted in the back rows of a bed or border, medium-height plants in the middle, and the shorter ones in front. In an island bed, tall flowers may be planted in the centre, with heights tapering down to the edges of the bed. Such a well-ordered bed not only shows all the flowers to their best advantage, but helps ensure that every plant gets the daily sunshine it needs in order to thrive.

In length of life, flowers fall into three groups: annuals, biennials and perennials. Annuals complete their entire life cycle in a year. The seeds or seedlings are put into the ground in the spring; the flowers germinate, grow and bloom; then the plants die in the autumn. Biennials have a two-year life span. They spend their first year germinating and growing, their second growing and flowering.

Perennials live for three or more years. Their hardy roots live underground all winter and send up new growth in spring.

Colours for All Seasons

A bed for a sequence of blossoms. The flower bed shown on the right in spring, summer and autumn produces colour in all three seasons and includes evergreen foliage for the winter months. It consists chiefly of perennials, including some spring bulbs for extra colour. A similar sequence of displays can be achieved with many different combinations of flowers, including annuals and biennials, if the plants are chosen for a wide range of flowering seasons.

In this example, the clematis and cotoneaster along the back wall bloom in the spring *(right, above)*. The peonies in the middle row and the candytuft in the foreground are also in bloom, along with bulbs: tulips, daffodils and hyacinths.

In summer *(right, centre)*, the climbing rose, tall phlox, and loosestrife provide colour at the back of the bed. The middle row is especially rich in plants that bloom, including the gayfeather, day lily, rudbeckia, common yarrow, speedwell and bergamot. At the front of the garden, the coral bells create a low border of attractive foliage and colour, and the tiny blossoms of the cotton lavender sharply define the front edge of the bed. At this point in the year, the plantain lily has large, richly coloured leaves and the miscanthus, a type of ornamental grass, is about 1.5 metres tall; neither will bloom until later.

In the autumn *(right, below)*, the roses still bloom, but the Japanese anemones have become the major feature of the bed. Day lilies continue to bloom into September and the miscanthus produces large white plumes. Plantain lilies provide colour through the middle of the bed. The carnations may continue to bloom and the autumn chrysanthemums are in flower. The cotoneaster will have bright red berries in the autumn and winter, and an autumn-blooming species of clematis will add colour.

Although some bulbs must be dug up in the autumn and stored over the winter, they too are technically perennials.

Flowers can be bought at a nursery or garden centre or ordered from the bumper crop of catalogues mailed out every winter. When buying plants, look for healthy green leaves, stocky stems and a good root system. It is tempting to purchase plants in full bloom, but those with few flowers are usually fresher and better. Bulbs should be firm and free of blemishes or mould.

Set out perennials and annuals in the spring, in beds that have been prepared in advance. To grow perennials from seed, start them indoors in pots or trays well before spring. Annuals grow faster, and depending on how hardy they are, can be grown in trays *(pages 54–55)* or sown outdoors, directly in the ground. Hardy bulbs should be planted in the autumn to bloom the following spring; tender bulbs should be planted in spring to bloom later in the year. To plant bulbs, set them pointed end up at the depth specified on the package or, if no directions are given, at a depth equal to twice the height of the bulb.

In autumn, annuals must be dug up and disposed of; a compost heap *(page 35)* is the ideal place. Perennials reappear without having to be replanted, but they do need some care at the end of the season. Every two or three years—when the blooms begin to get less vigorous—dig up the plants and divide them using the method for propagating ground covers on page 57. If the central part of a perennial has died, discard that portion and replant the healthy stems from the edges of the clump. After two or three frosts and at a time when the top of the soil is frozen, cover sensitive perennials with a layer of mulch to insulate the ground; this blanket of mulch interrupts the freeze-thaw cycle that causes the earth to heave and break roots in severe winters.

Preparing Perennials for the Winter

Cutting and covering the plants. After two or three frosts, cut the foliage of herbaceous, or fleshy, perennials about 50 mm above the ground with hedge clippers or secateurs. In cold areas cover the stubs with a light layer of evergreen cuttings, pine needles or straw. Woody perennials should be pruned to remove dead foliage and flowers, but they do not require mulch.

Two Ways of Planting Bulbs

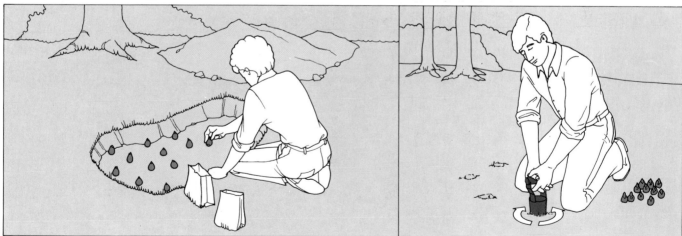

Bulbs by the bed or singly. To make a bed of bulbs, dig out the soil to a depth 25 mm greater than the planting depth recommended for the bulbs. Work a mixture of fertilizer and humus into the soil in the bottom of the bed and on a clay soil add horticultural grit to improve drainage. Spread some of the excavated soil 25 mm deep over the mixture and press the bulbs into the soil, wide end down and about 125 mm apart *(above, left)*. Sprinkle the remaining soil over the bulbs, smooth the surface and water the bed.

To plant single bulbs, dig a hole for each bulb with a trowel or a bulb planter *(above, right)*. Mark the planter with tape at a point 25 mm higher than the correct planting depth. Insert the planter into the earth and twist it until the tape reaches the surface. Lift the tool to pull out a core of soil. Mix some fertilizer and grit into the soil in the hole, then put back about 25 mm of soil. Set a bulb in the hole, and replace the remaining soil. Dampen each bulb location; replace the turf.

4

The Finishing Touches

A garden fountain. A whimsical frog tosses a decorative arc of water towards a small garden pond. Precast in a variety of materials ranging from inexpensive plastic to costly bronze, hollow fountain figurines can be fitted with a small pump and a length of plastic tubing to add a charming focal point to any garden.

By themselves, plants can usually supply almost anything needed for a landscaped garden, from grassy lawns to tree-shaded living areas, from shrubby foundation plantings to walls and trellises covered with climbers. But a man-made garden structure often makes a crucial addition to a landscape. Such a structure can provide a showcase for unusual plants or establish an arresting vantage point from which to take in the landscaping plan. The great estates of the past employed such elaborate devices as ornate gazebos, shimmering reflecting pools and colonnaded loggias to dazzle and awe visitors. Large-scale flourishes of this kind are rare in modern gardens, which tend to be on a more intimate scale, but even modest efforts can produce remarkable results.

Water and rock, for example, are elements that, separately or in combination, can enhance the beauty of any garden. Important components of garden layouts for centuries, pools and fountains continue to weave their spells wherever they are used. Modestly scaled pools of concrete or plastic, set into or above the ground, are easy to install *(pages 100–101)* and can serve as habitats for goldfish and aquatic plants while mirroring the colours of sky, trees and flowers. A small pump and some plastic tubing—both surprisingly easy to install—can transform a piece of hollow garden statuary into a fountain or create a miniature waterfall cascading down a rockstrewn slope *(pages 100–110)*.

Even without a waterfall, a rock garden has its uses and its beauty. It provides an answer to such problems as rock outcrops, steep slopes or an isolated patch of ground separated by a path or driveway, because each of these sites can be converted into a rock garden, subdued or spectacular. The garden could be made up of nothing more than a blanket of ivy, concealing or softening the jagged contours of exposed boulders. Or it might be a striking centrepiece, with a complex pattern of slopes and terraces adorned by unusual or very decorative plants.

While rock gardens command attention by lifting small plants a little way above the garden floor for better display, such structures as trellises, pergolas and archways *(pages 116–121)* flaunt fast-growing climbers at eye level and higher. Few garden sights can match the colourful explosion of rambler roses in full bloom on a trellis, or a frieze of wisteria blossoms dangling from the rafters of a free-standing pergola. The simple but sturdy support structures have an added attraction: they are almost as pleasing to the eye in winter, when they stand bare, as they are during the growing season, when they are largely concealed by their burdens of blossoms and foliage.

Working with Water in Pools and Fountains

For centuries landscape architects have complemented plantings with the soft reflections of a quiet pond or the dramatic arc of a fountain. Either effect can be created in a shallow, one-piece fibreglass pool, set into a hole dug to match its moulded shape. A typical small pool is about 2.5 metres long by 1.5 metres wide and 600 mm deep; most models come with a rounded rim, which can be blended with its surroundings by an apron of shrubs, ground covers or gravel. Pools are generally available in aqua blue, black or brown; most landscape designers prefer the dark colours, which confer an illusion of depth. Even the pool's actual, shallow depth can present a hazard to infants and young children. Protect them with a low fence round the pool.

For a home owner who wants the serenity of a still pond, a submerged recirculating pump placed on its side will move the water enough to keep it from stagnating, without disturbing the surface. The same pump, with slightly different plumbing, can also power a prefabricated fountain. Some fountains are simple arrangements of pipes that shoot a jet of water straight up into the air or produce a lacelike, arching spray. Others conceal their piping in statuary, which rises from the water of the pool or stands outside the rim and sprays water inwards.

The electric pump that powers a fountain draws in water through a screened intake to protect the mechanism from debris, and discharges it through a pipe; if the fountain itself is outside the pool, the pipe is linked to the pump by a flexible outlet hose. An electric cable and the hose can be draped over the edge of the pool or snaked through a hole drilled in the pool wall. For the first arrangement, spray-paint the clear plastic hose black to camouflage it; for the second, use a plastic-based clay to plug the hole round the cable and hose.

Although a pump must be small enough to remain inconspicuous in a shallow pool, it must also have enough pumping capacity to keep a fountain flowing strongly and steadily. To help determine the size of pump you need, you must know two figures: the total vertical distance, called the lift, between the outlet of the pump and the level at which water is discharged into the air; and the volume of water in your pool.

The pump you order should be able to lift that volume in a reasonable amount of time; ask the pump supplier for advice on this. For example, an adequate fountain pump recirculates all of the water in a 2.5 by 1.5 metre pool (about 800 litres) in about one hour with a lift up to 1.6 metres. It is better to buy a pump that delivers a little more water than necessary; the flow rate can be reduced by narrowing the outlet hose with a clamp or by crimping the end of the discharge pipe with pliers.

Bringing electricity to your pool is the trickiest part of a fountain installation. By digging trenches and laying cable yourself, you will save considerable expense, but you should always call in an electrician to make the final connections.

Electrical regulations concerning safety procedures for new installations stipulate that garden equipment must never be plugged into a standard unprotected socket outlet, and that a circuit supplying garden equipment must be protected by a residual current circuit breaker (RCCB)—a safety device that switches off the power when it detects a very small leakage of current to the earth. Modern domestic circuits are usually already fitted with a circuit breaker; if not, have one fitted as near as possible to the consumer unit. Some submersible pumps run off the main 220/240 volt domestic current, as shown on these pages. Other models work on a lower voltage, and require a transformer.

The simplest installation method is to use PVC-insulated, PVC-sheathed cable, run through a plastic conduit, buried deep enough to avoid any damage from subsequent digging or planting. A depth of 500 mm will normally be sufficient, although you should dig deeper—up to 900 mm—under a vegetable plot, where disturbance from digging will be greater. The position of any underground cable should be marked on the surface with marking tape or cable tiles. At the point where the cable enters the house, fit a back outlet terminator, shown on page 102—a weatherproof enclosure that can be opened to ease the cable round the bend.

It is possible to connect your pump to the underground cable with a simple waterproof connector, but an outdoor socket at this point will serve the same purpose, and can be used for other garden appliances as well. The socket must have an index of protection of at least 44 (look for IP 44 in the specifications) and should be fixed firmly to a wall or post (never to a fence) at least 75 mm above the ground.

With the pool installed and the pump and fountain in place, maintenance consists essentially of periodic drainage and cleaning. For drainage, let the recirculating pump do the work; simply detach the pump outlet hose from the fountain. The best way to keep pool water sweet-smelling and relatively clear (a certain amount of cloudiness is inevitable and natural) is to stock the pool with fish and aquatic plants *(page 104)*, along with a population of snails and tadpoles to help maintain an ecological balance.

Installing the Pool

1 Excavating and levelling the pit. Dig a pit to the approximate shape and depth of the pool. Level the pit every 300 mm, using a 100 by 50 mm piece of timber with one end set on the edge of the excavation and the other end on an offcut of wood as long as the pool is deep. Check the timber at each point with a spirit level, and add or remove soil wherever necessary. Finally, spread 25 to 50 mm of sand over the bottom of the pit, and smooth the sand evenly with a trowel or spade.

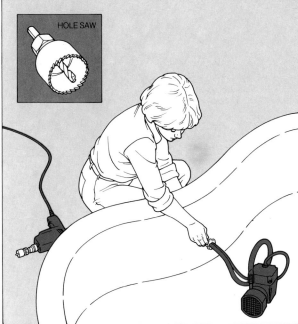

HOLE SAW

2 Running a cable and hose into the pool. Although the electrical cable and outlet hose of the pump can simply be draped over the side of the pool, you may prefer to conceal them. Drill a hole through the side of the pool below the water line, using a portable electric drill fitted with a 50 mm hole saw (*inset*), then place the pump on the bottom of the pool, and thread the hose and the electric cable out through the hole. Working from both sides of the pool wall, plug the hole round the cable and hose with plastic clay.

3 Setting and filling the pool. With a helper, lower the pool on to the sand bed, then add or remove soil if necessary to bring the pool rim 25 to 50 mm above ground level. Fill the pool with water from a garden hose; at the same time, backfill soil against the pool sides to equalize the pressure on the thin fibreglass walls. Finally, shovel loose soil under the outer lip of the rim.

Preparing to Bring Electricity to the Pool

1 Making an exit from the house. Dig a narrow trench 500 mm deep, extending from the house to the position of the outdoor socket. At the house, drill a hole through the wall above floor level, wide enough to take a section of conduit. Using a hacksaw, cut a piece of conduit long enough to reach from the hole in the wall to the bottom of the trench, less 75 mm. Fit one end of the conduit to the side spout of a back outlet terminator. Cut a second length of conduit to the thickness of the wall; fit one end to the central spout of the outlet terminator, and push the other end through the hole. Fit the end of the conduit inside the house to the central spout of a second back outlet terminator *(inset)*; if necessary, cut the conduit to ensure a tight fit. Cement the ends of the conduit to the spouts with conduit solvent. Secure the conduit to the exterior wall with saddles.

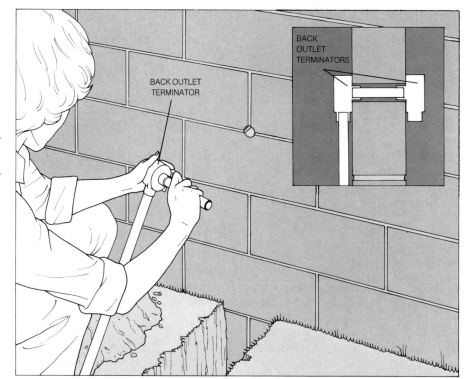

2 Feeding cable to the inside. Cut a piece of PVC-sheathed cable long enough to run from inside the house to the outside socket. Unscrew the lids from both outlet terminators. Push one end of the cable up through the conduit from the trench into the external back outlet terminator. Bend the upper end of the cable to push it through the conduit in the wall and out through the side spout of the back outlet terminator inside the house. Screw the lids back on both terminators and seal the exterior one with a gasket.

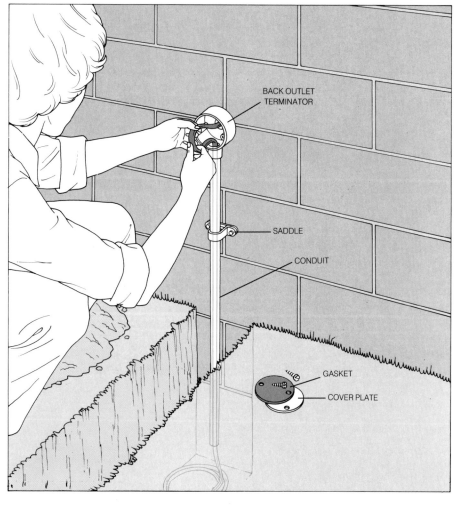

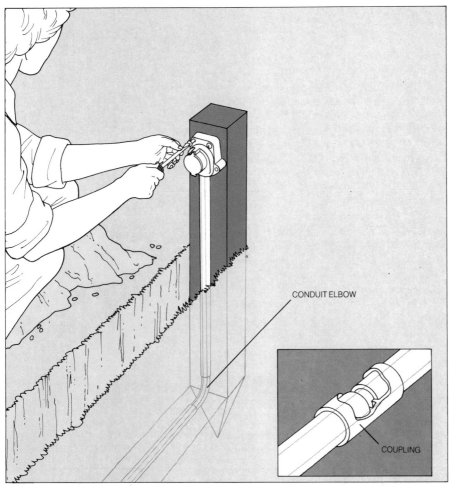

3 **Installing the outside socket.** Feed the cable through a right-angled conduit elbow and then through lengths of straight conduit along the trench. Connect the separate sections of straight conduit with couplings *(inset)* and cement the joints with solvent. At the end of the trench, feed the cable through a second right-angled conduit elbow and then through a vertical section of conduit rising at least 75 mm above ground level.

Call in an electrician to connect the cable to an RCCB inside the house and to a weatherproof socket at the end of the vertical section of conduit. Drive a timber stake treated with preservative into the bottom of the trench adjacent to the vertical conduit, then screw the weatherproof socket to the stake. Keep the electricity circuit switched off while you are working. Fill in the trench, packing soil tightly round the stake and vertical conduit to hold them in place.

CONDUIT ELBOW

COUPLING

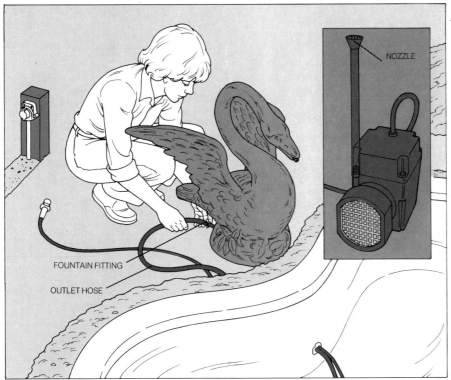

4 **Hooking up the pump.** To connect the pump to a freestanding fountain, thread and clamp the pump's outlet hose to the pipe fitting in the fountain, usually located at the back or bottom of the base. Plug the pump's electric cable into the outdoor socket and use the RCCB switch in the house to start the pump.

If you prefer a simple jet or spray in the pool rather than a separate fountain, do not use an outlet hose. Instead, screw a vertical length of 12.5 mm threaded pipe directly to the pump outlet, and install a nozzle at the top of the pipe *(inset)*. The type of nozzle you choose will determine the shape of the jet or spray.

NOZZLE

FOUNTAIN FITTING

OUTLET HOSE

Aquatic Plants for a Healthy Pool

Even a shallow garden pool affords the home gardener the chance to cultivate aquatic plants. Some, such as the water hyacinth, float on the surface; others, the hardy water lily, for example, generally grow in soil packed in submerged containers. Such plants are useful as well as decorative, keeping the water clear and sweet smelling. In a pool that contains fish, aquatic plants are especially important; they release oxygen underwater and inhibit algae growth.

Submerged oxygenating plants such as the common fishweed keep algae in check by using up the mineral salts in the water, starving the algae: allow one for every 0.2 square metres of pool surface. Floating plants discourage algae growth by blocking out sunlight. Marginals, the plants that grow round the pool's edge, are used mainly decoratively. Irises, flags and water hawthorn are good choices.

Techniques for planting aquatics vary. Floating plants can simply be tossed into the pool; they will grow roots down to the pool bottom without any help. Most water lilies and marginals, however, must be planted in containers on the pool bottom. If this submerges the young plants too deeply, prop the containers up so that no more than 75 mm of water covers the growing tips of the plants; then, as the plants send out new stems and leaves, lower the containers to the bottom.

Do not cover more than half the surface of a pool with plants. A medium-sized lily will cover up to a square metre, a smaller variety half a square metre or less. Aquatics should be planted during the growing season from May to August. They can be bought ready planted or you can plant them yourself in perforated plastic containers *(below)*.

When cold weather sets in, you can leave both plants and fish in the pool, so long as ice does not extend down to the plant roots. If the pool is shallow and winters in your area are severe, net the fish and transfer them to an indoor aquarium filled with water from the pool. Then drain the pool and move the plant containers into an unheated basement or garage. A covering of dampened moss peat will provide adequate moisture. When warm weather returns, clean the pool, refill it and return the fish and plants to their usual outdoor habitat.

Pool and plant care is minimal during the growing season. You may need to top up the pool occasionally—with rainwater rather than tapwater—to replace evaporated water, and you will have to trim dead leaves and flowers, and cut back rampantly spreading foliage.

Planting aquatics. The garden pool shown below illustrates the planting positions of the various types of aquatic plants. Plant the roots of water lilies and marginals in containers lined with hessian or clipped turf, and filled with 50 mm of moss peat, 225 mm of rich, clay soil and 25 mm of pea gravel *(inset)*. Do not use a container made of copper, which is toxic to fish; any other material is acceptable. For most species of water lily, the ideal size of container is 450 by 500 mm, but miniature varieties can thrive in 150 mm pots.

GRAVEL

SOIL

HESSIAN

MOSS PEAT

WATER LILY

FLOATING PLANT

DEEP MARGINAL

MARGINAL

SUBMERGED OXYGENATING PLANT

Embellishing a Garden with a Homemade Waterfall

Much as a fireplace and a crackling fire enliven a room, a waterfall enhances a garden. The basic components of a home-built waterfall are a pond at the base of a slope, a reservoir or discharge pool at the top, a trough running between the two, and an electric pump that circulates water round the system. But when the parts are disguised with rough stone, and the water flows and falls, this construction has the appearance and sound of a scene formed entirely by nature.

The simplest waterfall to build begins with a natural slope beside an existing garden pond. The slope, in fact, is all but essential; if your garden does not contain a pond, you can install a fibreglass pool as shown on pages 100–103. In most other respects, the size and shape of the waterfall are limited only by your imagination. Study natural waterfalls for ideas. Also consider the points from which you want to look at the waterfall. Then outline the positions of the trough and discharge pool on the ground with powdered chalk.

With the pool in place and the waterfall plan marked out on the ground, determine the size of pump you will need. A garden waterfall should circulate between 400 and 1500 litres of water an hour. Measure the total height of the fall—this is the vertical distance from the bottom of the fibreglass pool to the top of the trough—and order a pump that will lift 400 to 1500 litres per hour to that height.

The shells of the trough and discharge pool consist of pre-mixed concrete which is trowelled on to beds of gravel and reinforced with steel mesh. A 40 kilogram bag of concrete will make 0.014 cubic metres, enough to cover about 1400 square centimetres spread 100 mm thick. To determine the areas of the shells, measure the trough and the discharge pool separately, then add 10 per cent to allow for the extra area created by the pool's depth.

Both of the concrete shells are painted with a thin layer of masonry bonding agent, then coated with a 25 mm-thick layer of black waterproof mortar; the mortar not only makes the surfaces leakproof, but serves as a bed for the decorative stones. You will need enough mortar to cover the entire surface of the trough and pool, and an additional quantity to bond the stones in place. It takes about 0.028 cubic metres of mortar spread 25 mm thick to cover one square metre.

Mix the concrete and the mortar separately in a mortar pan, stirring them with a shovel. To mix the concrete, pour a bag of pre-mixed concrete into the pan and add just enough water so that a handful will barely hold together in a clump. To make 0.028 cubic metres of mortar, mix 50 kilograms of fine builders' sand together with 8 kilograms of Portland cement and 500 grams of black cement pigment (sometimes called carbon black), then add enough water to make a stiff mixture that will stick to a trowel held upside down.

Stone for the waterfall itself and for the camouflage of the concrete shell can be obtained from a stonemason. Or you may purchase it from a quarry; many quarries will also deliver the stone to the site, but you can cut costs by transporting it yourself. Handle all stone carefully to prevent nicks and breaks that can spoil the weathered appearance.

Pre-mixed concrete, Portland cement, cement pigment, wire reinforcing mesh, masonry bonding agent, gravel and builders' sand are all available from builders' merchants. You will need a few specialized tools: a bricklayer's trowel, a float and a jointing tool. If you have to cut stones to fit, you will also need a stone chisel and a short-handled mallet called a maul. Always wear heavy gloves and strong boots when you are working with concrete, mortar or stone and, if you cut stones, wear safety goggles to protect your eyes.

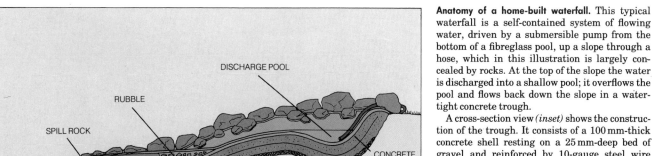

Anatomy of a home-built waterfall. This typical waterfall is a self-contained system of flowing water, driven by a submersible pump from the bottom of a fibreglass pool, up a slope through a hose, which in this illustration is largely concealed by rocks. At the top of the slope the water is discharged into a shallow pool; it overflows the pool and flows back down the slope in a watertight concrete trough.

A cross-section view *(inset)* shows the construction of the trough. It consists of a 100 mm-thick concrete shell resting on a 25 mm-deep bed of gravel and reinforced by 10-gauge steel wire mesh. It is coated with a 25 mm layer of waterproof mortar. The trough channels water to the fall—which consists of a stone wall backed up with rubble, and a flat spill rock. Water pours over the lip of the spill rock, which is cantilevered 125 mm over the edge of the lower pool. The rims and surfaces of both the trough and the discharge pool are camouflaged by rocks and pebbles, all set in a bed of waterproof mortar.

Building the Concrete Shells

1 **Digging the trough and the pool.** Mark the outlines of the trough and discharge pool with powdered chalk sprinkled on the ground. At the side of the fibreglass pool, and within the boundary lines, dig the fall's footing, consisting of a 125 mm-deep, level excavation which extends 200 mm from the pool's edge; shovel the excavated soil on to a piece of canvas or into a wheelbarrow for later removal. Then, working up the slope from the footing, dig a trench with gently sloping sides to the planned depth of the stream plus 125 mm for the concrete shell and its mortar coating. At the top of the slope, dig the discharge pool 50 to 75 mm deeper than the trench and with similarly sloping sides. Finally, pour a 25 mm-deep layer of gravel into the trough and the discharge pool.

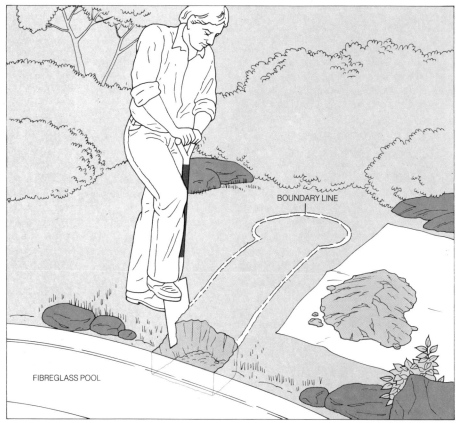

BOUNDARY LINE

FIBREGLASS POOL

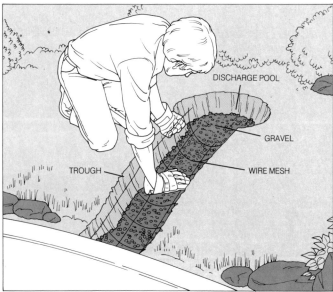

DISCHARGE POOL

GRAVEL

WIRE MESH

TROUGH

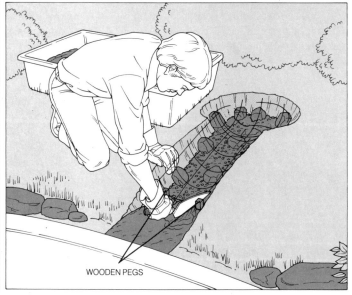

WOODEN PEGS

2 **Laying wire reinforcement.** Measure the sides and bottom of the trough with a flexible measuring tape, cut a section of reinforcing steel mesh to fit, and press the mesh into the trough, shaping it to the contours of the excavation. In the same way, cut and shape a section of mesh to fit the discharge pool.

Set pieces of brick or stone beneath the mesh to raise it 50 mm above the gravel bed. Mix the concrete and water in a mortar pan.

3 **Building the footing.** Drive four wooden pegs into the ground just inside each corner of the 200 mm excavated footing area beside the fibreglass pool. Mark off a height of 100 mm on each peg, and trowel concrete into the area to that depth to provide a footing for the stones of the fall. Remove the pegs as you go, and fill in the holes with more concrete.

4 **Shaping the concrete shells.** Working in sections 600 to 900 mm long, trowel a 100 mm layer of concrete into the trough *(below, left)* gauging the depth against pegs as in Step 3; at the rims of the excavation, build the concrete up to about 25 mm above the level of the surrounding ground.

Trowel a concrete shell for the discharge pool in the same way. Using your gloved hands, shape the concrete rims of the trough and pool into a single, continuous rounded lip *(below, right)*. Use the tip of the trowel to smooth out any irregularities on the concrete's surface.

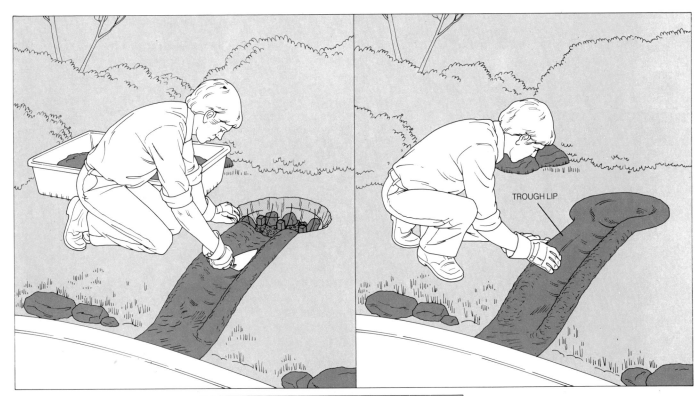

TROUGH LIP

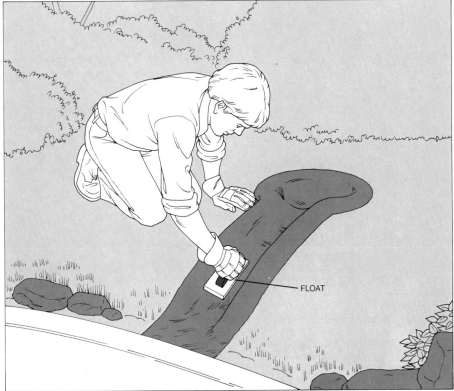

FLOAT

5 **Finishing the surface.** Skim a wood float over the concrete, pressing down just enough to smooth the surface. Begin at the centres of the trough and the pool and work up the sides, compacting the concrete and pushing out all the water that rises to the surface.

Adding the Stonework

1 **Applying a waterproof mortar base.** Using an old 75 mm-wide paintbrush, spread a layer of masonry bonding agent over the surface of the trough and the discharge pool *(right)*. Let the bonding agent dry until it is tacky to the touch.

Mix a batch of dark-coloured waterproof mortar and, using a bricklayer's trowel, coat the trough and pool with a 25 mm layer of mortar. Let the mortar cure for at least three hours.

While the mortar is curing, set the stones you will use for the waterfall on the ground, with their good sides up, so that you can find the right stone for the right place at a glance.

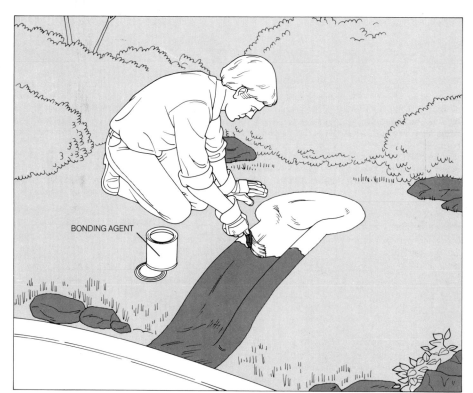

BONDING AGENT

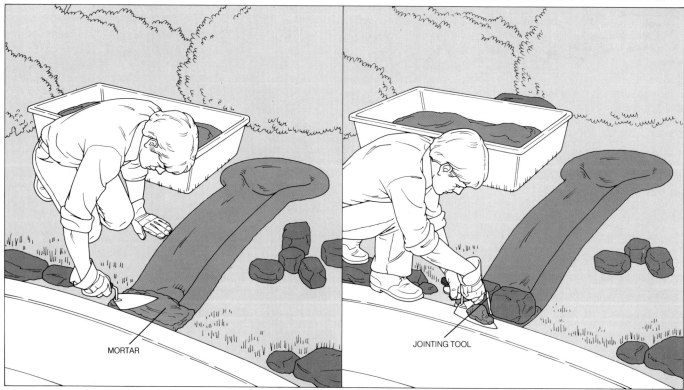

MORTAR

JOINTING TOOL

2 **Building the fall.** From a second batch of mortar, trowel a 25 mm mortar bed on the concrete footing *(above, left)*. Select a large, flat-bottomed stone, paint its base with bonding agent and set the stone firmly in the mortar bed. Trim away excess mortar with the trowel. Set a second large stone beside the first, leaving a 12 mm gap between the two; fill the gap with mortar, using the trowel as a palette and pushing mortar from it with a jointing tool *(above, right)*, until the mortar is compacted tightly between the stones. Lay a 12 mm bed of mortar on top of the two stones. Coat the base of another flat-bottomed stone with bonding agent and set it in the mortar, overlapping the joint between the bottom stones; set two more stones on either side to complete the course. Lay successive courses of stone to build the wall up to the desired height. It is important that the stones should be fairly uniform in shape; if your stones are not uniform, use a cold chisel and maul to chip off any irregularities.

3 **Laying a base for the rubble.** Spread a 25 mm bed of waterproof mortar on the trough, starting just behind the stone wall and extending up to a point level with the top of the wall. To find this point, set a level on the wall with one end touching the bottom of the trough. Slide the level up or down the slope of the trough until the bubble is centred in the glass tube of the level.

4 **Backfilling with rubble.** Select enough small and medium-sized stones to fill the area behind the wall. Paint the base of each stone with bonding agent and set it in the mortar bed, separating the stones by about 12 mm on all sides. Trowel mortar into the spaces between the stones and compact it with a jointing tool.

Spread another 12 mm coat of mortar on top of the rubble and set in more stones. Continue this procedure until you have built up a flat surface of rubble and mortar extending back into the trough and level with the top of the wall.

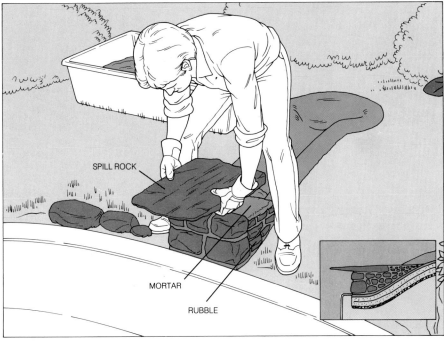

5 **Setting the spill rock.** Spread a 12 mm bed of mortar over the top of the stone wall and the rubble fill. Set the spill rock in the mortar, with one edge of the rock cantilevered out over the edge of the wall to project at least 125 mm over the edge of the fibreglass pool. Fill the area just behind the spill rock with mortar and small chunks of rubble, then coat the top of this rubble with mortar to form a smooth, even surface that is level with the top of the spill rock *(inset)*.

6 **Completing the stonework.** Line the opposite edges of the spill rock with stones, forming two low walls to direct water straight over the fall. For this part of the job, paint the base of each stone with bonding agent, set it in its own mortar bed and fill in joints *(page 108, Step 2)*.

Continue setting stones along the edges of the trough and, if you wish, you can put small stones in the trough, working your way up the slope; set the final stones on the bottom and round the rim of the discharge pool.

7 **Raking the joints.** After the mortar has set for one to two hours, use a jointing tool to rake out the joints between stones and round the base of each stone. Rake out mortar until the joints are barely visible, but leave enough to hold the stones securely. Clean off any spatters of mortar with a wet stiff-bristled brush. Scatter pebbles or gravel on the floor of the trough to cover any exposed mortar. Install the pump, pump wiring and plumbing, as demonstrated on pages 100–103, and fill the upper and lower pools.

Rock Gardens: Rugged Frames for Alpine Displays

An ordinary garden is a sort of botanical still life, often elegantly artificial. By contrast, a rock garden is a wilderness area in miniature. Like a landscape painter, a rock gardener achieves a natural effect by recasting nature subtly, placing rocks and tiny plants to simulate a mountain landscape. On a steep slope a rock garden has the practical virtue of substituting for grass, but even on a flat site a raised-bed rock garden, as shown on pages 113–114, can be an intriguing visual feature.

Careful planning is particularly important, because both rocks and the alpine plants typical of rock gardens are difficult to reinstall. Sketch an overall design on graph paper, then test its visual effect by staking out the rock locations with sheets of newspaper. Exploit your garden's natural topography by building the rock garden round any existing rock outcrops. Because alpine plants require particularly good drainage, they are generally planted on steep slopes; drainage is further improved by a planting base of porous rubble or gravel topped by a sandy soil mixture. Most species require a certain amount of sunlight but do not tolerate a baking heat. If possible, orient the garden so that it is shaded from the midday sun, but try to avoid positioning it under dense trees

which would obscure the light and also shed their leaves on to the plants.

The garden's rocky skeleton should look natural and unobtrusive, so choose a single type of local, neutral-coloured stone, if possible porous enough to retain moisture. Widely used are sandstone and grey limestone, which is ubiquitous and inexpensive but has one drawback: acid-loving plants must be planted above it on a slope, because the alkaline lime can leach into the ground below. Other possibilities include gneiss, granite, shale, schist and tufa.

The best source of rocks is a local quarry. You can have stone delivered by the tonne, but a bulk load will contain many unusable rocks; it is usually better to take away selected stones from the quarry yourself, or to pick stones for later delivery.

For the most part, avoid small rocks, which tend to clutter a garden; also avoid rounded stones, which often look artificial. Look for a few big, irregular rocks of the desired shape—flat ones for a ledge or a wall, boulders for an isolated outcrop. By using the techniques on pages 23–24, two people can safely handle quite large stones; those weighing more than 100 kilograms must be placed in a prepared bed *(pages 112–113)* by a professional crane operator.

Having selected your site, treat the area

with a long-life residual herbicide several weeks before starting work. Before you start digging holes and placing stones, schedule the job to suit your capabilities. A garden less than 2 metres square can usually be built and planted in two or three weekends, but a larger one may be best assembled step-by-step. This approach is particularly important in a raised-bed garden, where plants are set in during construction rather than afterwards.

The traditional plants for a rock garden are dwarf alpine species that grow above the tree line, but many gardeners now substitute hybrid cousins that flourish nearer to sea level. The garden's mainstays are exuberant clusters of tiny wild flowers, available from garden centres and by mail order. The tiny scale of the plantings and the garden's lean soil exclude most sea-level flowers, but a few other lowland plants such as herbs and dwarf shrubs, or succulents in hot climates, fit naturally into a rocky setting. Once planted and topped with gravel, the garden requires regular weeding, the control of snails and slugs, and an occasional watering if the leaves begin to wilt during periods of dry weather. Light pruning may be necessary for fast-growing plants or those that produce straggly growth.

An understated alpine habitat. Rocks are a natural, unobtrusive setting for this garden's true centrepiece, an array of tiny alpine plants. An artful, apparently random design mimics natural rock formations, with large, deeply embedded rocks that suggest ledges and outcrops.

Specimens are planted in their natural locations—succulents in crevices, for example, and trailing flowers on ledges—but the planting position also reflects the desired visual effect. Because most alpine plants are less than 200 mm tall, dwarf trees are not planted in their natural location at the bottom of a slope when they might block the view. Plants of a single species are grouped together to avoid clutter and heighten visual contrasts. Positioning also anticipates each plant's growth cycle, so that the garden remains visually balanced as flowers and foliage change with the seasons *(chart, page 115)*.

TRAILING FLOWERS

DWARF CONIFER

SUCCULENTS

Building a Rock Garden on a Slope

1 **Preparing the drainage bed.** Using a spade, strip all turf off a section of the slope up to 2 metres square, then dig up about 450 mm of soil from the section. Reserve the turf and soil in separate piles for later use.

To provide proper drainage, fill the bottom of the section with 150 mm of broken bricks or rocks. Cover this rubble with pieces of the original turf, grass side down *(right)*, or with stone chips or coarse sand; such materials prevent soil from clogging the drainage bed.

RUBBLE

TURF

2 **Preparing the soil.** If your soil is particularly unstable, support the rocks that will project above the soil by setting flat, 100 mm-thick rocks 300 to 600 mm apart on the drainage bed. Mix 2 parts of coarse sand with 1 part each of topsoil, leaf mould and fine gravel. Fill the excavation with the mixture, completely burying the flat rocks, and rake the surface level with the surrounding grade. Thoroughly wet the bed with a hose and let the soil settle for a week or so, then remove any weeds that have appeared and fill any low spots with more of the soil mixture.

Arranging Rocks in Formation

Planting rocks in a slope. For each rock, dig a step in the slope deep enough to accommodate at least one-third of the rock's bulk; shape the step so that the rock's broadest side will face down and its top will tilt into the slope, draining water back into the soil. Pack soil firmly round the rock, then stand on the rock and shift your weight to test its stability; if it moves, embed the rock more deeply. Plant the biggest rocks first, working from the bottom of the slope to the top; then sparingly plant a few small rocks in the same way.

Building a rock outcrop. Select several thick, flat rocks with similar lines of horizontal strata and vertical fractures. Plant the bottom rock, tilting its top into the slope; the angle can vary from slight to extreme, according to the garden's design. Cover the top of the rock with about 18 mm of soil mixture; then, one by one, dig steps for succeeding rocks and stack them above and behind the first, securely embedding each in the slope and topping it with a very thin layer of loose soil. Align strata and fracture lines wherever possible; if necessary, adjust a rock's angle by inserting chips of stone beneath it. Hose away soil from the exposed faces of the rocks, then trowel soil into the crevices and plant them with specimens that thrive in dry soil.

STRATA LINES

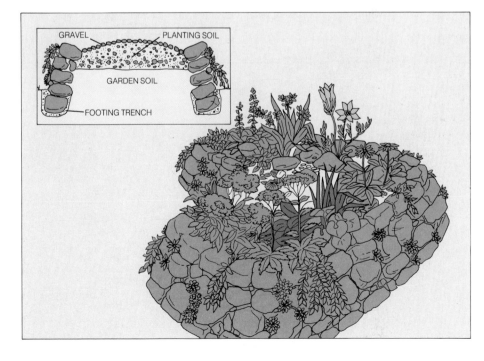

GRAVEL   PLANTING SOIL

GARDEN SOIL

FOOTING TRENCH

A Rock Garden for a Level Site

Anatomy of a raised-bed garden. Although rock gardens are traditionally built on slopes, a similar effect can be achieved on level ground by constructing stone walls that raise a garden bed 600 or 900 mm above the ground, ensuring proper drainage. Built up over shallow footing trenches *(inset)*, the mortarless walls slope inwards for stability; crevices between stones are packed with soil and plants. The basin formed by the wall is often filled with earth, topped by a deep bed of planting soil and 50 mm of gravel; a planter less than 600 mm deep is often entirely filled with planting soil. In both cases the level of the filling is as high as possible to allow for later settlement. Together the walls and bed create an effective setting for various alpine plants *(chart, page 115)*.

Building a Walled Garden Bed

1 Laying the foundation. Mark the wall's outer boundary with stakes and string. Just inside the string, dig a footing trench 150 to 300 mm deep and slightly wider than the largest stone slabs. Lower these slabs into the trench, tilting each slightly inwards and butting the stones snugly together so that their tops form a smooth shelf. Pack earth round this course of stones and cover it with 12 mm of an alpine planting mixture—2 parts of coarse sand and 1 part each of garden topsoil, leaf mould and fine gravel.

2 Building the walls. Lay subsequent courses of square rocks, staggering the vertical joints to prevent erosion and setting each course slightly within the one below it. As the wall rises above the ground, check its inward slope with a home-made slope gauge. To make the gauge, nail 50 by 25 mm scraps of timber to form a right-angled triangle, consisting of a short horizontal side, a long vertical side and a longer diagonal; the horizontal side should measure about 50 mm for every 300 mm of the vertical one. When a level shows that the vertical side is plumb—or perfectly vertical—the diagonal side will be at the correct angle for the slope of the wall.

Compensate for uneven or wobbly rocks by using thicker layers of soil and by inserting chips of stone. Set plants at intervals in the crevices. If your soil drains poorly, line the basin inside the wall with gravel; reinforce any weak sections of the wall by bracing boulders against its inner face. As you work, fill the basin inside the wall with earth and tamp it firmly against the sides; use planting mixture for the top 250 mm of the bed. The soil level should be 50 to 75 mm higher than the top of the wall to allow for settlement. After rooting seedlings in the bed, cover the exposed soil with 50 mm of gravel mulch.

SLOPE GAUGE

A Selection of Rock-Garden Plants

	Soil		Light			Height			Growth habit			Special traits			Flower colour			
Plants Suitable for a Rock Garden	Acid	Alkaline	Shade	Partial shade	Full sun	Under 150 mm	150 to 300 mm	Over 300 mm	Upright	Spreading	Trailing	Flowers	Foliage	Evergreen	White-green	Yellow-orange	Pink-red	Blue-purple
ANEMONE NEMOROSA (**wood anemone**)	●			●	●		●					●			●		●	●
ARENARIA MONTANA (**mountain sandwort**)	●			●	●					●	●	●			●			
ARMERIA MARITIMA (**sea pink**)				●		●		●				●		●	●		●	
CAMPANULA CARPATICA (**Carpathian bellflower**)				●		●	●		●			●			●			●
CERATOSTIGMA PLUMBAGINOIDES (**leadwort**)				●			●			●		●	●					●
CHRYSOGONUM VIRGINIANUM (**goldenstar**)	●		●			●	●	●	●			●				●		
DIANTHUS GRATIANOPOLITANUS (**Cheddar pink**)				●		●		●				●			●		●	
DICENTRA EXIMIA (**fringed bleeding heart**)	●		●				●	●				●	●		●		●	
EPIMEDIUM GRANDIFLORUM (**epimedium**)			●				●					●	●		●	●	●	●
HELIANTHEMUM NUMMULARIUM (**rock rose**)		●		●		●		●		●	●	●			●	●		
IBERIS SEMPERVIRENS (**evergreen candytuft**)		●		●		●			●			●		●	●			
IRIS LACUSTRIS (**dwarf crested iris**)	●			●	●	●		●				●			●			●
IRIS PUMILA (**dwarf bearded iris**)		●				●		●				●			●			●
PHLOX DIVARICATA (**wild blue phlox**)	●			●		●			●			●			●			●
PHLOX SUBULATA (**moss phlox**)			●	●		●				●		●			●		●	●
PRIMULA SIEBOLDII (**Siebold primrose**)	●			●		●		●				●			●		●	●
SAPONARIA OCYMOIDES (**rock soapwort**)			●			●				●	●	●					●	
SILENE SCHAFTA (**catchfly**)			●			●		●				●					●	
TIARELLA CORDIFOLIA (**foam flower**)	●		●			●		●				●			●			

	Soil		Light			Height			Growth habit			Special traits			Flower colour			
Plants Suitable for a Raised Bed	Acid	Alkaline	Shade	Partial shade	Full sun	Under 150 mm	150 to 300 mm	Over 300 mm	Upright	Spreading	Trailing	Flowers	Foliage	Evergreen	White-green	Yellow-orange	Pink-red	Blue-purple
AETHIONEMA x WARLEYENSE (**'Warley Rose'**)		●		●	●			●				●	●	●			●	
ANDROSACE SARMENTOSA (**rock jasmine**)				●	●			●				●	●				●	
ANEMONELLA THALICTROIDES (**rue anemone**)	●			●			●		●			●			●		●	
ARMERIA CAESPITOSA (**thrift**)		●		●	●		●					●		●			●	
CAMPANULA PORTENSCHLAGIANA (**Dalmatian bellflower**)		●		●	●					●		●						●
DIANTHUS ALPINUS (**alpine pink**)		●		●	●		●					●			●		●	
DRABA AIZOIDES (**whitlow grass**)		●		●	●					●		●				●		
DRYAS OCTOPETALA (**mountain avens**)				●	●					●	●	●	●	●	●			
ERIGERON AUREUS (**fleabane**)				●	●		●					●				●		
ERYTHRONIUM DENS-CANIS (**dog-tooth violet**)	●			●		●		●				●			●		●	●
GENTIANA ACAULIS (**trumpet gentian**)		●		●		●			●			●						●
GYPSOPHILA REPENS 'FRATENSIS' (**creeping baby's breath**)		●		●	●					●	●	●					●	
HEPATICA TRILOBA (**hepatica**)			●		●			●			●			●			●	
HUTCHINSIA ALPINA (**alpencress**)			●		●			●		●	●		●				
IRIS GRACILIPES (**Alba iris**)	●			●		●		●			●			●				●
LEWISIA COTYLEDON (**cotyledon lewisia**)			●				●			●	●	●		●		●	
PRIMULA FARINOSA (**bird's eye primrose**)		●	●			●		●		●		●			●		●	
SAXIFRAGA PANICULATA (**saxifrage**)		●	●			●			●		●	●	●		●			

Choosing plants for rock gardens. The top half of this chart lists plants suitable for planting in a rock garden; the bottom half lists plants which are recommended for raised beds. In both sections, plants are listed by their scientific Latin names in alphabetical order followed by their most common English names. All the plants in this chart are tolerant of frost. Dots in the Soil and Light columns indicate the best growing conditions for each plant; the absence of a dot in the Soil column means that a plant can thrive in either type of soil, acid or alkaline. Heights given include the height of flowers, if there are any. Dots in the columns for Growth habit, Flower colour and Special habits indicate other significant physical features; more than one dot in any of these columns means that the features can vary within a single species.

115

Trellises and Pergolas for Climbing Plants

If left to grow untrained, most climbing and trailing plants will ramble aimlessly across the ground, over fences or up walls. They look better and are easier to care for when they are specially grown for display on trellises, pergolas and archways. Such structures can also enhance attractive features of the landscape, such as patios and garden paths, or conceal unattractive elements, such as toolsheds and dustbins.

The simplest support for garden climbers is a trellis, upon which a plant can be trained to grow vertically and horizontally. Trellises come in many sizes and shapes, from lightweight structures of thin wood strips called laths, to massive frames and bulky grids for such heavy climbers as vines and wisteria. The trellises can be erected singly or in series against a wall, at right angles to a fence or doorway, or as freestanding dividers or centrepieces.

A trellis mounted horizontally on a set of posts becomes a pergola *(pages 118–119)*, providing a pleasant, sun-dappled shelter; the sides can be enclosed with vertical trellises or left open to sun and breeze. A pair of vertical trellises joined by an arch *(pages 119–121)* becomes an elegant gateway.

Designing and building a trellis, pergola or archway need not be difficult or complicated. A few basic construction rules ensure that the structure will be sufficiently sturdy and well anchored to support a full-grown climber and withstand high winds or frost heaves.

Wall-mounted trellises should be built with frames or spacers that hold the plants at least 50 mm away from the wall. This clearance permits air to circulate behind the trellis and prevent damage to a climber from heat reflected off the wall.

To support freestanding trellises, pergolas and archways, set sturdy posts 450 to 600 mm deep. It is usually not necessary to anchor the posts in concrete; just tamp the soil round the posts firmly. For particularly heavy structures, on the other hand, add concrete to each post hole for extra stability *(page 118, Step 1)*.

Trellises and other climber supports can be made from a wide variety of materials, from plumbing pipes to galvanized steel wire and plastic rope; the traditional and most common material is wood. Naturally weather-resistant woods, such as oak and cedar, are the most attractive, but also the most expensive. Less costly are softwoods, such as hemlock and douglas fir, pressure-treated, stained or painted to resist rot. Wood that touches or enters the ground— the support posts of a freestanding trellis, for example—should be further protected with a non-toxic wood preservative, such as copper naphthenate. Treat cut ends of timber in the same way, and bevel the top of vertical posts to help water run off quickly.

Building a trellis can generally be done with a few basic tools—a saw and a hammer or staple gun will usually suffice. Hardware for outdoor construction is inexpensive and readily available; use galvanized steel or aluminium nails, staples, hinges and so on to avoid rust stains.

Nearly all climbers will grow well on a trellis or pergola if the soil at the base is moderately moist but well drained. A few climbers, notably Boston ivy, may be adversely affected by the alkalinity of lime seeping from nearby concrete or concrete-block foundations; either correct the soil with annual additions of sulphur compounds *(page 32)* or substitute alkaline-tolerant plants such as clematis.

As young climbers begin to climb a trellis, tie the stems loosely to the supports with a soft, moisture-resistant material, such as raffia, garden cord or even strips cut from old nylon tights. Secure plants from the base upwards *(page 61)*, and check periodically that the ties are not restricting growth. As perennial climbers mature and fasten themselves securely to the supports, the ties can be discarded.

A Sampler of Trellises

A hinged trellis. Vertical and horizontal 50 by 25 mm slats, nailed together in a grid pattern, are mounted on 75 by 75 mm posts to provide support for heavy, bulky climbers. Spacers and sets of hooks and eyes hold the trellis 150 mm from the house wall; a pair of strap hinges, fitted into the posts *(inset)*, permit the entire structure to be folded down if access to the wall is required.

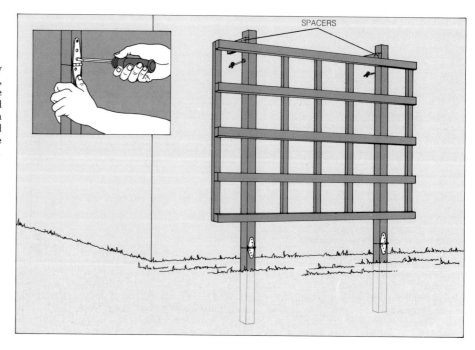

SPACERS

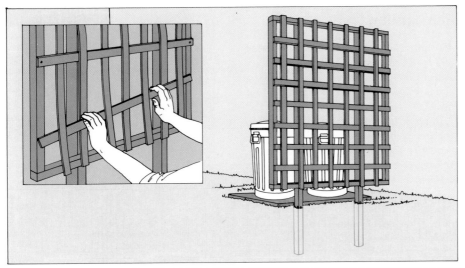

A basket-weave trellis. In a trellis especially suitable for light climbers, 50 by 10 mm slats are woven together and nailed to a frame of 50 by 50 mm timbers. To create the basket-weave pattern of slats, nail the tops of the vertical slats to the frame, at least 75 mm apart, then weave the horizontal slats through the vertical slats *(inset)*, working each one upwards to form a row of open squares. As you set each horizontal slat into position, nail its ends to the frame; when you have positioned the last horizontal slat, nail the bottoms of the vertical slats to the frame. Finally, nail the frame to 75 by 75 mm posts in front of a wall or, as shown here, as a freestanding unit.

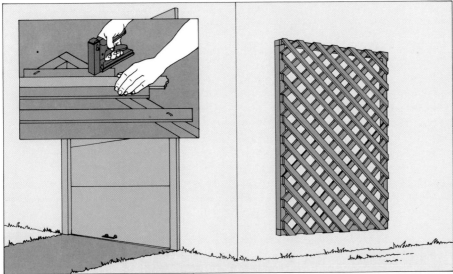

A latticework trellis. The diamond-shaped pattern of this latticework trellis can be assembled with strips of narrow lath for lightweight climbers or with thicker, stronger slats for heavy plants. To simplify laying out the criss-cross strips, use one strip as a spacing device *(inset)*. Staple or nail the ends of the strips to a 50 by 50 mm frame, then trim the parts of strips projecting beyond the frame with a jigsaw or circular saw, and nail the entire trellis to a wall, using masonry nails, or to posts as above.

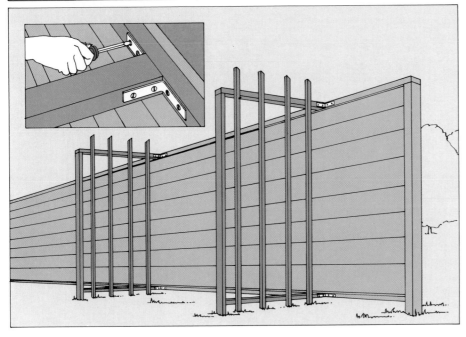

A wing trellis. Set at right angles to a fence or wall, a wing trellis serves as an informal space divider. The trellises shown here consist of vertical 25 by 25 mm battens nailed to three-sided 100 by 50 mm frames. The horizontal members of the frames are fastened to a fence by pairs of galvanized angle brackets *(inset)*. The vertical posts rest on the ground; no digging is required.

Espaliers: Touches of Whimsy for the Garden

Normally, trellises are not needed to support a bush or a tree, but they can be used to impart whimsical, two-dimensional shapes to such non-climbing plants as fruit trees, flowering quince or forsythia. The creation of such displays as the candelabrum shown on the right is part of an ancient art form called espalier, which attained widespread popularity in the highly stylized formal gardens of 18th-century Europe.

Trellises for espaliers are generally wall-mounted rather than freestanding, with horizontal slats beginning about 450 mm above the ground and spaced 300 to 400 mm apart. It is not necessary to have vertical slats, as upward-growing stems support themselves and do not need to be restrained.

In order to create an espalier, position the tree or bush directly underneath the centre of the espalier trellis and prune the main stem back so that it is 50 to 100 mm below the bottom slat of the trellis. As the plant grows, tie its lateral shoots to the slats to force horizontal growth; cut off any shoots that cannot be trained to grow in the desired pattern.

Building a Post-and-Beam Pergola

1 Setting the posts. Dig four holes up to 2.5 metres apart for the 100 by 100 mm posts of the pergola. Make each hole about 300 mm wide and 450 mm deep; compact the soil in the bottom using a length of timber. Set each post into its hole and align it with the planned building line. As a helper holds each post upright and checks with a level that it is vertical, nail two temporary 75 by 50 mm braces at least 1500 mm long to adjoining surfaces of each post; anchor these braces to short stakes in the ground. Using a fairly dry concrete mix of 1 part cement to 5 parts combined aggregate, fill the holes round the posts to within 40 mm of ground level and tamp down the concrete firmly with a length of timber. Cover with soil and leave for three days to cure before completing the pergola.

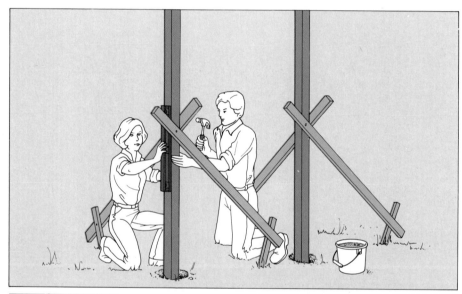

2 Mounting the beams. Check that the tops of the posts are level, and trim off any that are too high. Cut two pairs of beams from 225 by 25 mm boards, allowing for an overhang of at least 300 mm at both ends of the pergola. With the aid of a helper, raise each beam to the top of the posts, level the beam and nail it temporarily to the posts. After each pair of beams has been levelled and nailed to the opposite sides of a pair of posts, drill two 12 mm holes through the beams and each post. Run 150 mm coach bolts through these holes, and secure the bolts with washers and nuts *(inset)*. Cut spacers 100 to 150 mm long from scraps of post timber; nail them between the double beams, flush with the top edges, at intervals of 300 to 450 mm.

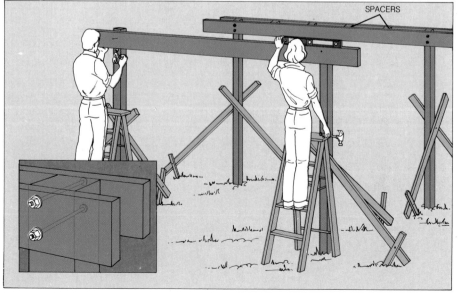

SPACERS

3 **Installing the rafters.** Measure and mark rafter positions on the tops of the beams at equal intervals up to 600 mm. Cut rafters from 150 by 25 mm boards, allowing for at least 300 mm of overhang on both sides of the pergola. Position each rafter edgewise on its marks, and toenail it to the beams from both sides. If toenailing is difficult, secure the rafters to the beams with metal rafter anchors *(inset)*, which can be obtained from builders' merchants.

An Optional Trellis Grid

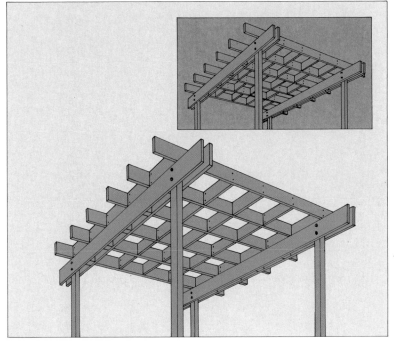

Filling the spaces between rafters. To brace the rafters of a pergola against twisting under a load of heavy climbers, and to increase the shade provided by the pergola, create a grid with 150 by 25 mm crosspieces set at right angles between the rafters. Mark the rafters for crosspieces at regular intervals from the inner beam on one side of the pergola to the inner beam on the other. Install one set of crosspieces between every other pair of rafters, nailing directly through the rafters into the ends of the crosspieces; toenail the remaining crosspieces to the faces of the rafters. Alternatively, stagger the crosspieces in a pattern *(inset)* that makes toenailing unnecessary.

Building an Arch of Trellises

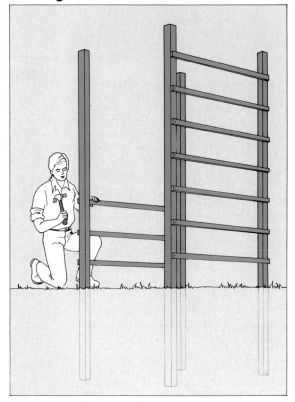

1 **Putting up the support posts.** Mark positions for front posts 600 to 900 mm apart if you plan to install a gate, 600 to 1500 mm apart otherwise; position the rear posts 600 to 1200 mm behind the front ones. Put up all four posts *(opposite, Step 1)*, using 100 by 100 mm timbers that rise at least 1.8 metres above the ground. At intervals of 200 to 300 mm, nail 50 by 25 mm strips up the sides of the archway; the last strip should be about 150 mm from the top of the posts.

2 **Making an arch template.** On a sheet of cardboard, draw a horizontal line equal to the distance between the outside edges of the posts. At each end of the line, measure in the actual width of the 100 by 100 mm posts; indicate these points with short vertical marks. Nail or pin one end of a length of string to the centre of the horizontal line, tie the other end of the string round a pencil and, with the string held taut, draw one semicircular arc between the ends of the line and another between the short vertical marks. Cut out the arch template with a trimming knife.

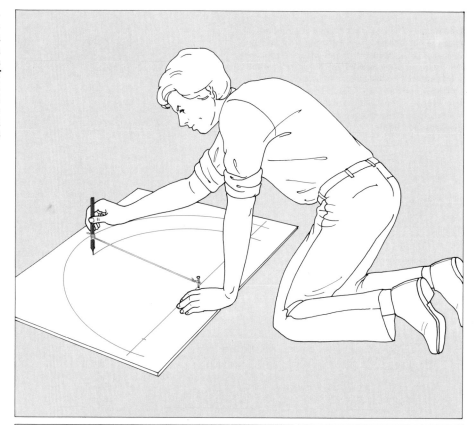

3 **Cutting out the arches.** Arrange three 225 by 25 mm boards into a rough arch on which you can lay the entire template; set a long board at the top, resting on the two side boards. Mark and cut the side boards along the lines at which they meet the long board, so that the three pieces abut each other. Trace the arch on the boards and cut it out with a jigsaw. Assemble and cut three more sets of boards in the same way.

Cut four more arches with the same template. For this second set of arches, place long boards at the sides of the arch (inset), rather than the top, so that the joints will be staggered when all of the arch segments are assembled.

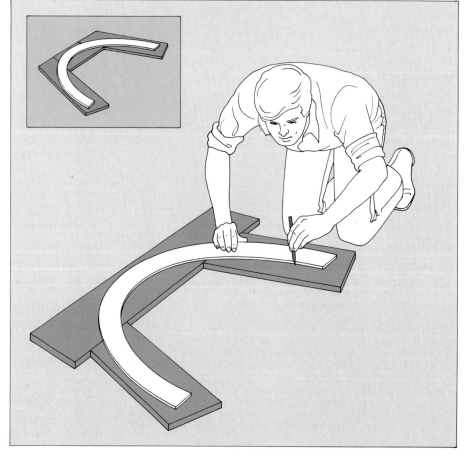

4 **Building two-layer arches.** Align a pair of arches—one from each set, so that the joints are staggered—and fasten them together with a waterproof adhesive and 30 mm nails. Repeat this procedure three more times so that you end up with four two-layer arches.

5 **Assembling four-layer arches.** Align two double-thick arches so that adjoining layers do not have the same joint pattern, and fasten these four-layer arches with adhesive and 60 mm nails. Trim and smooth the curved surfaces with a spokeshave and plane the flat ends if necessary.

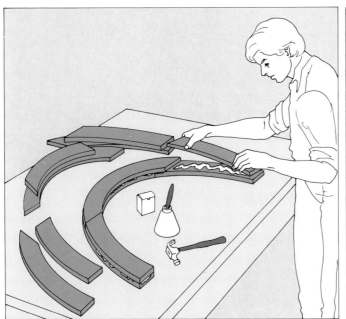

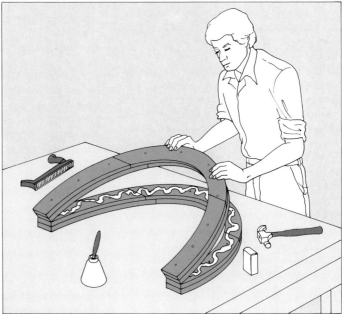

6 **Setting the arches.** Drive a panel pin half way into the top of each of the two front posts and cut off the heads with pincers. With a helper, align the front arch on the posts and tap it down *(left)* so that the cut ends of the panel pins mark drilling holes in the ends of the arch. Remove the arch. Take the pins out of the posts and, using a 9 mm bit, drill holes 25 mm deep into the ends of the posts and arch. Cut two pieces of 9 mm dowelling each slightly less than 50 mm long and fix the dowels into the ends of the posts using waterproof glue. Smear the post and arch surfaces with glue and tap the arch down on top of the posts to make a dowel joint *(inset)*. Toenail the joint for extra strength. Mount the rear arch flush with the back of the rear posts in the same way. Finish the pergola by nailing 50 by 25 mm strips over the top of the arches at the intervals established for the posts *(Step 1)*.

121

A Check List of Seasonal Chores

A landscaped garden requires year round care to stay healthy and beautiful, and each season calls for its own set of chores. Spring is a time of planting and preparing for the coming season of heavy growth. In summer, the gardener must maintain fast-growing lawns and beds with watering, weeding, trimming and cutting. Autumn chores consist mainly of preparation for winter but usually include some planting as well. And winter in cold climates means protecting plants from ice and snow, and planning for the coming spring.

You cannot rely solely on the calendar to mark the divisions between seasons. For the most part, use changes in temperature, weather and soil conditions as a guide. Changes in temperature and in the relative lengths of day and night are obvious clues. Spring comes after the danger of hard frost has passed, when bulbs begin to put out shoots, and perennial plants unfurl new leaves and stems. Summer is the heart of the growing season—the time of the highest temperatures and the longest days of the year. Autumn approaches as days shorten and temperatures drop; in temperate climates the season has arrived when the night-time temperature dips regularly to 13°C or below. Winter—the period when most plant growth slows down or stops entirely—has the shortest days and lowest temperatures of the year.

Changes in soil and growing conditions are more subtle. If you are unsure of the clues that mark the seasons in your area, ask your local garden centre or experienced gardeners for advice.

In the check list that follows, the essential chores for each season are named in a brief list. More information about these tasks is given in the paragraphs below. You will find detailed instructions for each job by referring to the index and the preceding pages of this book.

EARLY SPRING

REMOVE WINTER COVERINGS
CLEAN UP WINTER DEBRIS
RENEW MULCH
FEED GROUND COVERS
SPRAY DORMANT TREES
PRUNE SHRUBS AND ROSES

When the last heavy snows of winter have melted away, remove hessian or other protective coverings from shrubs and plants. Any late snows will probably not be heavy enough to damage branches. Pull old mulch away from the base of shrubs and rake leaves and other debris off the lawn and ground covers.

After this clean-up, mix the old mulch into the soil and lay new mulch around shrubs. Fertilize ground covers; run hedge clippers over ground cover beds to eliminate stringy top growth.

Before many leaf buds open, spray trees and shrubs with tar oil or an all-purpose spray for pest control. Prune summer and autumn-flowering shrubs that bloom on the current year's growth. Early spring is also the time to begin a general pruning of non-flowering shrubs and trees and to do the hard spring-pruning of roses.

In the flower garden, plant new perennials and fertilize old ones. Once there are signs of growth in the lawn, reseed any bare spots, then spread slow-acting lime and fertilizer over the entire expanse of grass and water it.

MID-SPRING

CUT GRASS
TRANSPLANT SHRUBS AND TREES
PULL WEEDS

Mid-spring marks the start of the repetitive maintenance tasks that your plants will need throughout the growing season. Except in areas containing bulbs, a first cutting of the grass is needed with the mower set at its highest level; and a pre-emergent weedkiller should be applied to the lawn. Do not cut the foliage of bulbs that have finished their flowering in early spring until the leaves have withered; alternatively, between six and eight weeks after flowering, dig up choice bulbs for storage until the autumn.

In both the lawn and planted beds, weeding should begin on a weekly basis. When the soil is dry enough to work easily, you can plant or transplant most trees and shrubs, both deciduous and evergreen. (A second opportunity for planting trees and shrubs will come in the autumn.) Mid-spring is also the time to plant, or divide and replant, small bulbs such as snowdrops, to flower the following year.

LATE SPRING

PLANT ANNUALS
MAINTAIN FLOWERING SHRUBS

Plant any remaining perennials and all of your annual seeds or seedlings, along with tender bulbs, rhizomes or tubers, such as cannas and dahlias. Remove dead flowers from flowering shrubs, which encourages further blossoms, and prune the shrubs when all the blooms have faded. Check the lawn regularly to see if the soil needs more or less water than your normal watering programme is providing.

EARLY SUMMER

PERFORM GENERAL SPRAYING
PRUNE HEDGES
EDGE AND WEED

As spring gives way to summer, apply pesticides to control fungus, insects, disease and scale on all plants that are particularly susceptible. For the best results with roses, continue spraying them once a week throughout the growing season.

Shape hedges and borders, and remove faded blossoms from annuals to stimulate further bloom. If you have a pond, now is the time to plant delicate water flowers, such as water lilies.

MIDSUMMER

WATER
WEED
CUT GRASS LONGER

As the summer proceeds, a combination of strong sun, periods of drought and drying winds creates a danger of leaf scorch. Keep all plants watered well to prevent damage; take special care to give any trees and shrubs that were planted in the spring a periodic soaking. Weed flower and shrub beds, and continue to remove the faded blossoms from annuals and perennials. Divide any perennials that have finished blooming, discarding the dead centres; replant the good shoots.

To protect a lawn from summer heat, start cutting the grass roughly 25 mm longer than you did in spring, so that it will not burn out. Test the soil of the lawn to determine the conditioning that it will require in the autumn.

LATE SUMMER

SOW GRASS SEED
FERTILIZE LAWN
PERFORM SPRAYING IF NEEDED
ORDER BULBS

The shorter days and cooler nights of late summer signal the time to start new lawns or renovate old ones. This is also a time to watch for increases in any pest population severe enough to warrant a second application of pesticide. Examine your plants for possible iron deficiency caused by their summer growth spurt: if you see yellow leaves with dark green veins, feed the plants with an iron-rich fertilizer; check the soil pH and drainage.

Continue regular weeding and watering. Take care not to over water; moderating temperatures begin reducing the plants' moisture requirements.

Start to watch the advertisements of local nurseries. You can buy and plant autumn-flowering bulbs as soon as they come on the market in your area. Order spring-flowering bulbs such as daffodils.

EARLY AUTUMN

FINISH LAWN RENOVATION
TRANSPLANT TREES AND SHRUBS
PLANT BULBS
START COMPOST HEAP

Aerate the lawn, and scarify it if necessary. Continue to mow the lawn regularly as long as the grass keeps growing, although you can cut it shorter and less often once the heat of summer has broken; apply lime to the lawn if needed.

Autumn is a good time to dig up and move evergreen shrubs and trees or to plant new ones. Wait until the leaves of deciduous plants have fallen before moving them. Bare-rooted roses can be planted, as can spring-flowering bulbs. Be sure to water new plants regularly and mulch them lightly to help control weeds.

If you do not have a compost heap, autumn is an excellent time to start one; your general pre-winter clean-up will soon produce a steady supply of compostable vegetable tops, dead or dying annuals, fallen leaves and other items.

Feed the roots of trees, especially ornamental ones, and dig up tender tuberous bulbs, such as gladioli, for storage in a frost-free place over the winter.

LATE AUTUMN

RAKE LEAVES
PRUNE ROSES
CUT PERENNIALS
CHECK MULCH
BRING IN EQUIPMENT

Late autumn is the time for a last flurry of activity before winter. Leaves must be cleared from lawns and ground covers. Old needles shedding off pine trees must be raked up. (They make a good mulch for acid-loving shrubs.)

The last pruning of roses should be completed in time to prepare the plants for winter; cut off long stems, so that they cannot be whipped by winter winds. Cut down herbaceous, or fleshy, perennials, and cover the stubble with mulch to protect next year's shoots. Prune trees and hedges one last time, where necessary, before the winter sets in. Dig up annuals after the first killing frost.

Mulch should be renewed or repaired on all shrubs at this time. Use a pronged cultivator to stir up mulch that has become so compacted that air and water are unable to reach the plants.

Scrape dirt, rust and grass off the lawn mower. Remove the spark plug and drain out the oil and petrol from petrol-driven mowers, then replace the oil and store the mower. Empty, clean and store your fertilizer and pesticide sprayers.

Dig dead plants out and add them to the compost pile. Spread manure or rough compost. Turn over the soil with a spade or a cultivator, leaving it in large clods.

Close any irrigation systems, turn off outside taps and bring in garden hoses and tools for storage.

EARLY WINTER

PROTECT SHRUBS
TRIM EVERGREENS
REMOVE DEAD LEAVES
REPAIR TOOLS

If severe winter storms are common in your area, be sure to protect shrubs and delicate trees from the coming ravages of ice, snow and wind. Use evergreen clippings, such as those from a pine or spruce, to cover low shrubs; wrap medium-sized ones with hessian. Build a roofed shelter around the plants under the eaves of your house, to shield the branches from snow which may slide off the roof. Protect broad-leaved evergreen plants from transpiration—the evaporation of water through the leaves—with antitranspirant spray.

Trim hollies and other broad-leaved evergreens for indoor decorations; the pruning will improve the health of the plants as well. Rake leaves from lawns and perennial beds; matted leaves can choke lawn grasses and promote disease.

Check your garden tools at this point in the year to see if they need to be sharpened, repaired or replaced. Test soil from herbaceous borders and flower beds so that the results will be on hand in time for spring soil conditioning and planting.

MIDWINTER

KEEP PLANTS FREE OF SNOW
PRUNE ORNAMENTAL TREES
ORDER SEEDS, SHRUBS AND
PERENNIALS

During the dead of winter, the major chore is still to protect plants from the elements. Check and repair protective coverings frequently and, after each snow storm, gently shake or brush the snow from branches. Apply a second coating of antitranspirant to broad-leaved evergreens. When you are clearing paths and driveways, take care not to shovel snow on to bordering plants. Instead of using plant-killing salts to melt snow near lawns and gardens, use fertilizer or wood ashes.

After bad storms, cut broken branches from shrubs and trees. Order seeds, shrubs and perennials from mail-order catalogues for spring planting.

Picture Credits

The sources for the illustrations in this book are shown below. Credits for the pictures from left to right are separated by semicolons, from top to bottom by dashes.

Cover: Martin Brigdale. 6–11: Martin Brigdale. 12: Drawings by Hayward and Martin Ltd. 13, 14: Drawings by Graham Sayles. 15: Drawings by Hayward and Martin Ltd. 17–21: Drawings by Eduino J. Pereira. 23: Drawings by Hayward and Martin Ltd. 24: Drawings by John Massey (2) – drawings by Hayward and Martin Ltd. 25: Drawings by John Massey. 26–31: Drawings by Hayward and Martin Ltd. 33: Drawing by William J. Hennessy Jr. from A and W Graphics; drawings by Hayward and Martin Ltd. 34, 35: Drawings by William J. Hennessy Jr. from A and W Graphics. 36: Fil Hunter. 39: Drawings by Walter Hilmers Studios – drawing by Hayward and Martin Ltd.; drawing by Walter Hilmers Studios. 40: Drawings by Walter Hilmers Studios. 41: Drawing by Hayward and Martin Ltd. – drawings by Walter Hilmers Studios. 42, 43: Drawings by Walter Hilmers Studios. 44: Drawing by Walter Hilmers Studios – drawing by Walter Hilmers Studios; drawing by Hayward and Martin Ltd. 45: Drawing by Hayward and Martin Ltd. – drawings by Walter Hilmers Studios. 46: Drawing by Arezou Katoozian from A and W Graphics – drawings by Hayward and Martin Ltd. 47: Drawing by Hayward and Martin Ltd. – drawing by Arezou Katoozian from A and W Graphics. 50: Drawing by Arezou Katoozian from A and W Graphics. 51: Drawings by Arezou Katoozian from A and W Graphics – drawing by Hayward and Martin Ltd.; drawing by Arezou Katoozian from A and W Graphics. 52: Drawings by Arezou Katoozian from A and W Graphics. 54–57: Drawings by Adisai Hemintranont from Sai Graphis. 58: Drawing by Hayward and Martin Ltd. – drawing by Adisai Hemintranont from Sai Graphis. 61, 62: Drawings by Hayward and Martin Ltd. 64: Fil Hunter. 67–69: Drawings by Jennifer and John Massey. 70: Drawing by Jennifer and John Massey – drawing by Hayward and Martin Ltd.; drawing by Jennifer and John Massey. 71–73: Drawings by Hayward and Martin Ltd. 74, 75: Drawings by Jennifer and John Massey. 76, 77: Drawings by Hayward and Martin Ltd. 78: Drawing by Adisai Hemintranont from Sai Graphis – drawing by Hayward and Martin Ltd. 79–81: Drawings by Adisai Hemintranont from Sai Graphis. 85: Drawings by Hayward and Martin Ltd. 86: Drawings by Frederic F. Bigio from B-C Graphics except bottom by Hayward and Martin Ltd. 87–96: Drawings by Frederic F. Bigio from B-C Graphics. 97: Drawing by Frederic F. Bigio from B-C Graphics – drawing by Frederic F. Bigio from B-C Graphics; drawing by Hayward and Martin Ltd. 98: Fil Hunter. 101: Drawings by Frederic F. Bigio from B-C Graphics. 102: Drawings by Hayward and Martin Ltd. 103: Drawing by Hayward and Martin Ltd. – drawing by Frederic F. Bigio from B-C Graphics. 104: Drawing by Hayward and Martin Ltd. 105–110: Drawings by Frederic F. Bigio from B-C Graphics. 111: Drawing by Hayward and Martin Ltd. 112: Drawings by Elsie J. Hennig. 113: Drawing by Elsie J. Hennig; drawing by Hayward and Martin Ltd. – drawing by Elsie J. Hennig. 114–117: Drawings by Elsie J. Hennig. 118: Drawing by Elsie J. Hennig – drawing by Hayward and Martin Ltd. – drawing by Elsie J. Hennig. 119, 120: Drawings by Elsie J. Hennig. 121: Drawings by Elsie J. Hennig – drawing by Hayward and Martin Ltd.

Acknowledgements

The editors would like to thank the following: John Aldridge, London; Bridgedale, Leicester; Greg Callaghan, Sydney, Australia; Kate Cann, Guildford, Surrey; Clifton Nurseries, London; Neil Fairbairn, London; Fédération Française du Paysage, Paris: Nicole de Gouttes, Paris; David Haviland, London; Julia Howes, Paris; Hozelock-ASL, Aylesbury, Buckinghamshire; Ralph Klucus, Sydney, Australia; Marshall-Tufflex, Hastings, East Sussex; Merry Tiller, Stowmarket, Suffolk; Derek Patch, Forestry Commission, Wrecclesham, Surrey; Vicki Robinson, London; Selfridges Gardening Department, London; Helen Shulston MCSP, London; Nick Spall, London; Spear & Jackson, Wednesbury, West Midlands; Leslie Stokes, London; Peter Truffit, London; Christel Wiemken, Hamburg; Wolf Tools, Ross-on-Wye, Herefordshire.

Index/Glossary

Metric Conversion Chart

Approximate equivalents—length

Millimetres to inches		Inches to millimetres	
1	1/32	1/32	1
2	1/16	1/16	2
3	1/8	1/8	3
4	5/32	3/16	5
5	3/16	1/4	6
6	1/4	5/16	8
7	9/32	3/8	10
8	5/16	7/16	11
9	11/32	1/2	13
10 (1cm)	3/8	9/16	14
11	7/16	5/8	16
12	15/32	11/16	17
13	1/2	3/4	19
14	9/16	13/16	21
15	19/32	7/8	22
16	5/8	15/16	24
17	11/16	1	25
18	23/32	2	51
19	3/4	3	76
20	25/32	4	102
25	1	5	127
30	1 3/16	6	152
40	1 9/16	7	178
50	1 31/32	8	203
60	2 3/8	9	229
70	2 3/4	10	254
80	3 5/32	11	279
90	3 9/16	12 (1ft)	305
100	3 15/16	13	330
200	7 7/8	14	356
300	11 13/16	15	381
400	15 3/4	16	406
500	19 11/16	17	432
600	23 5/8	18	457
700	27 9/16	19	483
800	31 1/2	20	508
900	35 7/16	24 (2ft)	610
1000 (1m)	39 3/8		

Metres to feet/inches		Yards to metres	
		1	0.914
2	6′ 7″	2	1.83
3	9′ 10″	3	2.74
4	13′ 1″	4	3.66
5	16′ 5″	5	4.57
6	19′ 8″	6	5.49
7	23′ 0″	7	6.40
8	26′ 3″	8	7.32
9	29′ 6″	9	8.23
10	32′ 10″	10	9.14
20	65′ 7″	20	18.29
50	164′ 0″	50	45.72
100	328′ 1″	100	91.44

Conversion factors

Length	1 millimetre (mm)	= 0.0394 in
	1 centimetre (cm)/10 mm	= 0.3937 in
	1 metre/100 cm	= 39.37 in/3.281 ft/1.094 yd
	1 kilometre (km)/1000 metres	= 1093.6 yd/0.6214 mile
	1 inch (in)	= 25.4 mm/2.54 cm
	1 foot (ft)/12 in	= 304.8 mm/30.48 cm/0.3048 metre
	1 yard (yd)/3 ft	= 914.4 mm/91.44 cm/0.9144 metre
	1 mile/1760 yd	= 1609.344 metres/1.609 km
Area	1 square centimetre (sq cm)/ 100 square millimetres (sq mm)	= 0.155 sq in
	1 square metre (sq metre)/10,000 sq cm	= 10.764 sq ft/1.196 sq yd
	1 are/100 sq metres	= 119.60 sq yd/0.0247 acre
	1 hectare (ha)/100 ares	= 2.471 acres/0.00386 sq mile
	1 square inch (sq in)	= 645.16 sq mm/6.4516 sq cm
	1 square foot (sq ft)/144 sq in	= 929.03 sq cm
	1 square yard (sq yd)/9 sq ft	= 8361.3 sq cm/0.8361 sq metre
	1 acre/4840 sq yd	= 4046.9 sq metres/0.4047 ha
	1 square mile/640 acres	= 259 ha/2.59 sq km
Volume	1 cubic centimetre (cu cm)/ 1000 cubic millimetres (cu mm)	= 0.0610 cu in
	1 cubic decimetre (cu dm)/1000 cu cm	= 61.024 cu in/0.0353 cu ft
	1 cubic metre/1000 cu dm	= 35.3147 cu ft/1.308 cu yd
	1 cu cm	= 1 millilitre (ml)
	1 cu dm	= 1 litre see **Capacity**
	1 cubic inch (cu in)	= 16.3871 cu cm
	1 cubic foot (cu ft)/1728 cu in	= 28,316.8 cu cm/0·0283 cu metre
	1 cubic yard (cu yd)/27 cu ft	= 0.7646 cu metre
Capacity	1 litre	= 1.7598 pt/0.8799 qt/0.22 gal
	1 pint (pt)	= 0.568 litre
	1 quart (qt)	= 1.137 litres
	1 gallon (gal)	= 4.546 litres
Weight	1 gram (g)	= 0.035 oz
	1 kilogram (kg)/1000 g	= 2.20 lb/35.2 oz
	1 tonne/1000 kg	= 2204.6 lb/0.9842 ton
	1 ounce (oz)	= 28.35 g
	1 pound (lb)	= 0.4536 kg
	1 ton	= 1016 kg
Pressure	1 gram per square metre (g/metre^2)	= 0.0295 oz/sq yd
	1 gram per square centimetre (g/cm^2)	= 0.228 oz/sq in
	1 kilogram per square centimetre (kg/cm^2)	= 14.223 lb/sq in
	1 kilogram per square metre (kg/metre^2)	= 0.205 lb/sq ft
	1 pound per square foot (lb/ft^2)	= 4.882 kg/metre^2
	1 pound per square inch (lb/in^2)	= 703.07 kg/metre^2
	1 ounce per square yard (oz/yd^2)	= 33.91 g/metre^2
	1 ounce per square foot (oz/ft^2)	= 305.15 g/metre^2
Temperature	To convert °F to °C, subtract 32, then divide by 9 and multiply by 5	
	To convert °C to °F, divide by 5 and multiply by 9, then add 32	

Phototypeset by Tradespools Limited, Frome, Somerset
Printed in Spain by Artes Gráficas Toledo, S.A.

D. L. TO:1837-1985   X